YOUR

CHARACTER

IS YOUR

CULTURE

Praise For *Your Character Is Your Culture*

"This is not merely a healthy reminder of the crucial role of maintaining culture in any successful organization—it is a play-by-play of how to do it, using a play-by-play of how it has been done! The book is as engaging as this cultural climate he describes and was responsible to build, and I cannot recommend it enough."

David L. Bahnsen, Founder, Managing Partner, Chief Investment Officer, The Bahnsen Group

"I have just gone down memory lane reading Dave Sparkman's book *Your Character Is Your Culture*. Our UnitedHealth Group journey was intentionally led by our CEO and was a top-down effort with all executives engaged.

Dave captures our learnings, both positive and challenging. His Trail Markers are rich in content with clear examples of how we impacted culture throughout the organization.

Character, beliefs, values, and experiential learning were fundamental to our success and always tied back to our mission/purpose.

Culture brings out the best in people, both personally and professionally. I enjoyed my personal journey and learned a lot about myself through it. Enjoy the book's insights for your culture Journey."

Mary, Former UnitedHealth Group Executive

"Dave Sparkman's book was conceived in the business world, but its impact reaches far beyond. As a pastor, I found his insights on character and culture just as applicable to church leadership, families, and community life. These lessons aren't abstract theories, they're practical truths that show how transformed character transforms culture. Whether you lead a company, a congregation, or simply your own household, this book offers wisdom worth applying."

Pastor JD Larson, North Coast Church

"I've long admired Dave's conviction that culture defines what's possible. His work at UnitedHealth Group is a masterclass in how purpose-driven culture fuels strategy, growth, and people's best work."

Gary Thomson, CPA, Founder, Thomson Consulting, LLC

"Dave Sparkman's new book, *Your Character Is Your Culture,* draws on his deep experience at United HealthGroup to make a strong case for the connection between culture and performance. The book gives profound and practical insights into how to understand and transform the culture of any organization. This book is a must-read for any aspiring leader."

Professor Arthur V. Hill, PhD, CFPIM, The John & Nancy Lindahl Professor Emeritus, Carlson School of Management, University of Minnesota

"Our relationship with work is one of the most important aspects of our lives. In this book, Dave Sparkman wisely investigates why work culture is so persistently vexing, offering concrete steps to deal with common career challenges while reassuring us that, amid all the angst, there is indeed the possibility for both leaders and individuals to choose to act with character. An invaluable, insightful book."

Richard Leider, Founder, Inventure – The Purpose Company, Bestselling author, *The Power of Purpose, Repacking Your Bags, and Life Reimagined*

YOUR CHARACTER IS YOUR CULTURE

Lessons From UnitedHealth Group's Transformational Journey

DAVE SPARKMAN

YOUR CHARACTER IS YOUR **CULTURE**

Lessons From UnitedHealth Group's Transformational Journey

Printed in the United States of America.

The views and opinions in this book are those of the author at the time of writing this book, and do not reflect the opinions of Indie Books International, its editors, nor the official policy or position of UnitedHealth Group Incorporated, or any other organization mentioned. Examples of communication and behavior are provided for illustrative purposes only. Also, to protect the privacy of the former and current UnitedHealth Group employees involved, names, job titles, and other identifying details have been changed or omitted throughout this manuscript. Any similarity to actual persons, living or dead, is purely coincidental.

Neither the publisher nor the author is engaged in rendering legal or other professional services through this book. If expert assistance is required, the services of appropriate professionals should be sought. The publisher and the author shall have neither liability nor responsibility to any person or entity with respect to any loss or damage caused directly or indirectly by the information in this publication.

Hardcover ISBN: 978-1-966168-78-2
Ebook ISBN: 978-1-966168-52-25
Library of Congress Control Number: 2026901945

Designed by Melissa Farr, Back Porch Creative, LLC

INDIE BOOKS INTERNATIONAL®, INC.
2511 WOODLANDS WAY
OCEANSIDE, CA 92054
www.indiebooksintl.com

Contents

Foreword

While leaders obsess over metrics and milestones, the most powerful force shaping their legacy unfolds in a thousand small moments each day. The word, collectively, for those billion moments is called culture.

Ultimately, the culture of an organization is a misnomer—an illusion. The truth is that collective culture is simply the manifestation of every single individual throughout the organization. And it begins with the leader. While setting the culture is no small task—indeed a heavy lift—it is bred in the details of the everyday. Every single day.

A leader can't be everywhere, yet their investment in culture engages the next best thing—empowering each person, in each moment. That is why what Dave Sparkman shares, in this book you hold, is so very important. The work on culture can be treacherous territory. And any treacherous trail you walk is less risky and more enjoyable when you have a guide.

There has never been a time in human history where change has been so substantial, so transformative. The speed can be breath-taking, and the trajectory of that speed is exponential. Yet, while the winds of a hurricane can be dangerous and destructive—there is always peace in the eye of the storm. Culture is that steady, grounding place in the eye of the storm. It is the difference between destructive reactions or a consistent response.

Culture is what inspires an internal guidance rather than an external compliance. In fact, an organization's high cost of compliance is the unmeasured price we pay for not valuing and investing in organizational culture to begin with. I have learned from my business coach, Mark LeBlanc:

> *The little things you do every day are far more important than the big things you do every now and then.*

This book is designed to help you be a master of the consistency of those little things. No doubt, this is not easy. It is hard. Very hard—as most great things tend to be. Oh, it is easy to begin as some flavor-of-the-month initiative. But a transformational journey is a whole different story. Much like a trail, it will have its twists and turns, ever-changing weather and those moments where the next step seems impossible. That is where the leader keeps taking the next step forward for all to follow.

When it comes to a leader taking the responsibility for leading the culture, there is no finish line. The day you think you have arrived, is the day you squander the stewardship of all you will have accomplished. Dave Sparkman would be the first to tell you he did none of this alone—but I would be the first to tell you that he was both the spark and the pilot light along the way until his final day at UnitedHealth Group. I have known Dave Sparkman for decades. I have also experienced the depth of his gift to not only see what others fail to see—or choose not to see—as well as his courage, patience and persistence to guide others there. That is what you too will experience by walking this trail.

The culture you build today will outlast every strategy you implement. Dave hasn't just seen the map. He has walked this path and lit the way for you to follow. While there is no finish line, there is indeed a starting point. Your guide is waiting and inviting you on one amazing journey.

John G. Blumberg
Author of *Return On Integrity*

Preface

Why I Wrote This Book

My father was a pastor for over forty years, and I remember a sermon illustration he used multiple times. He explained how our new, converted nature wrestles with our old, fleshly nature for control over our thoughts and behaviors. The story goes like this:

In a small country town lived an old man who owned two dogs—a white one and a black one. The dogs would fight whenever they could touch each other. When asked which dog would win the fight, the old man responded, "Whichever one I feed the most." His reinforcement to all of us, "Are you feeding your old or new nature?"

My parents consistently emphasized how important individual character was. Doing the right thing reflected who you were as a person, and it didn't matter what my peers thought or what everybody else was doing. That was our household culture. Character was not a "one and done" event, but a fluid, ever-present striving to live out beliefs. I needed to be grounded in those beliefs, so when hard decisions came, I would not waver in that difficult situation. While I experienced (and still have) many shortfalls through my character development, I learned that how I treated others flowed from my beliefs and values.

Most of my thirty-five years working with people and workplace culture came from being employed at two stellar companies: Arthur Andersen and UnitedHealth Group.

Given what has occurred with both of those enterprises, you might be asking yourself, "Why would I read this book given the demise of Andersen and the current difficult times at UnitedHealth Group?"

I'd be asking the same question; however, as with many situations:

All is not as it may appear.

When I joined Arthur Andersen directly out of college, the firm was known as the Marines of the Big 8 accounting firms. I immediately felt the impact of the firm's seven Core values and credo of "think straight, talk straight." Highly ethical conduct accompanied exemplary client service as the norm. There *was* a correct way to do things at Andersen, and principled guidelines gave useful boundaries to empower our people for the myriad of daily judgment calls needed. Although acquitted years after being wrongfully indicted, the eighty-seven-thousand-person firm imploded in 2002 and never recovered.

Andersen gave me a high awareness of what living out corporate beliefs and values can do for organizational health. So when I joined UnitedHealth Group in 2003, I immediately saw and felt a stark difference from the culture I had just left. UnitedHealth Group was financially successful with wonderful people; however, the collective character was ill-defined, not a focus, and not aligned with the organizational mission and values. Everyone did their best, but the ever-shifting, demanding, and cutthroat environment hindered us from reaching our potential. It was then that our Chief Executive Officer placed a bet on culture in 2009.

This book chronicles lessons learned from UnitedHealth Group's cultural transformational journey from 2009 to 2018, when I served as the

SVP, Culture for UnitedHealth Group. My journey with UnitedHealth Group ended when I exited the organization in January 2019.

Motivated by Andersen's 2002 implosion, with many more insights gained from my experience at UnitedHealth Group, I've endeavored to investigate and demonstrate the value of investing in your people to gain a healthy workplace culture. Bottom line: by offering your people the opportunity to build lasting results individually, you'll collectively reap exponential benefits.

Most available articles and books on workplace culture have been written by consultants and academics. They usually have tremendous experiences with clients, or they've done extensive research on enterprises to prove out their theories. Many of the previously written books have interesting methodologies, intriguing stories, illustrative concepts, and catchy phrases to make their points. However, most of them have not had the ongoing experience of keeping the culture transformation journey going. While these books can be useful, few practically share proven tactics to sustain a cultural transformation.

Simply put, they have not had to live in the bed they made. I had to create and walk this path, live out the journey, and carry responsibility for workplace culture success.

While this book will hopefully be an interesting read for you, the primary purpose in writing it is to help you see what we experienced and learned along the way, with successes and failures in charting a course that proved to be transformational in the life of the enterprise. What we learned is marked with "Trail Markers" to help you potentially see where you are and where you might want to go next. You will notice that I primarily refer to my former colleagues by their job titles rather than their full names, and their names have been changed. This decision was made to honor the privacy of individuals and allow the focus to remain purely on the lessons learned during the culture transformation journey.

As a retreaded Certified Public Accountant (CPA) and a former certified Senior Professional Human Resources (SPHR) executive, most of my career was spent working to provide practical and tactical approaches to improve business performance. As a partner at Arthur Andersen and then a Chief Administrative Officer at UnitedHealth Group, my role rarely involved in-depth technical research or analytics. Typically, I found myself leveraging others' technical expertise and then working to enable people to perform at their best.

While you'll get a good feel for the flow and story of UnitedHealth Group's culture journey, I'm hopeful the insights gained may be useful for your organization. After seven years away, my perspectives and filters continue to evolve, shaping further ideas on how to ignite and fuel lasting results.

Ideally, you'll get the most from the book if you read it cover to cover, but if you're like me, you may go to a Trail Marker from the contents page that looks interesting to you and work it from there. Each Trail Marker can stand alone and doesn't have to be read with the others. But please understand, in the end, it's all systemically connected.

While my experience with workplace culture has been at two large organizations, I'd encourage you to remember a foundational truth: Inevitably, people are just people. While recognizing each organization and each person in them is beautifully unique, the need to define, align, and aggregate their collective characters to the organizational mission and values is critically important.

Thus, whether your organization is a group of four or 400,000, culture is advanced one person, one day, one step at a time.

Every person matters because a transformed character transforms culture.

Workplace culture is a journey that never ends.

In fact, based on my experience, the work must never end.

Dave Sparkman
Minneapolis, 2026

Trail Marker #1

Place Your Bets

"You miss 100 percent of the shots you don't take."
WAYNE GRETZKY

Little did the chief executive know the significance of the journey that lay ahead for his enterprise.

The time was April 2009. Robert was the Chief Executive Officer of UnitedHealth Group (UHG), a large healthcare company serving seventy million people with approximately 140,000 employees.

Revenues for the year would hit $87.1 billion, with net income landing at $3.8 billion. UHG is ranked No. 21 on *Fortune*'s list of the largest companies. By almost every key performance indicator, UHG is a large, high-performing company.

But on this day in early 2009, Robert was thoughtful and somewhat pensive. He has been working at the large conference room table in his office for hours, with his familiar twenty-one-column yellow spreadsheets neatly laid out around the table, and based on his eyes darting from one to the other, something is just not landing right for him.

Despite the promising forecasted numbers at play, something didn't feel right. Something he couldn't put his finger on kept him from getting comfortable with the pro forma approaches he'd drafted for UHG.

He sat back in his chair and reflected. The last few years since his appointment as CEO in 2006 had been a maelstrom, as he had been initially charged with cleaning up after a stock option scandal that led to his predecessor leaving the organization.

Additionally, the 2005 PacifiCare acquisition integration had not gone as planned. The significant customer losses and customer service issues that plagued UHG were not due to an overly sophisticated process but rather from simple failures to execute.

He also considered the scores of acquisitions UnitedHealth Group had made and would continue to make. Each one started out well, but like other companies all over the world, the integration efforts were never smooth. The mechanics worked, but the people issues never seemed to stop.

As his thoughts flowed back to the future, he contemplated the upcoming possibilities for what became known as Obamacare. While he didn't know many of the aspects and concerns Obamacare would ultimately carry, he knew business as usual would not be the case.

His mind wrenched back to the present, where it seemed like every day he had to deal with an unsettling level of silo mentality amongst UHG business segments in solving enterprise-wide problems. Despite hiring many bright people and continually sharpening strategic clarity, results were only achieved by fighting through ongoing bickering and divisive behavior. The root issues seemed so infantile. Why can't people just get along?

Somehow, some way, there had to be a path forward to enable UHG to achieve the potential he saw in the past and future. But something was missing. What could it be?

A few days later, he was sharing some of these reflections and concerns with James, a trusted former colleague from Arthur Andersen, the renowned accounting firm that had imploded from the Enron scandal back in 2002. James had been Andersen's CEO when Robert served as their chief financial officer, just before Robert left to join UHG in 1997.

James reminded Robert about one of Andersen's fellow partners, Dr. Larry Senn. After Andersen's implosion, Larry rejuvenated Senn Delaney, a corporate culture consulting firm that Andersen had previously acquired. They had helped Andersen and many other large corporations, and perhaps Larry might have some insights to help UHG.

Robert leaned into that advisement. While not his bailiwick, culture was something he knew was important. After all, Andersen's culture of "think straight, talk straight" was something important to him, and he had experienced it working. Shortly after he arrived at UHG, he developed "Rules of the Road," a set of attributes and principles he felt would be useful for all UHG executives. But where was that now? In a binder on the shelf. For some reason, it had not taken root.

When Larry and Robert met in July 2009, Larry listened attentively to the UHG history and to Robert's unsettling conclusion that something was missing. Larry pointed out to him that, despite having an exceptional business strategy and an organizational structure that could certainly support it, the UHG cultural foundation would not achieve the results Robert was targeting.

That explanation landed with Robert. To gain a competitive advantage and maximize UHG's potential, the missing piece might be culture. Not surprisingly, Senn Delaney had a methodology to address the dilemma of how to get after it.

Robert agreed to go through the transformation process Larry prescribed, beginning with his senior leadership team and himself participating in an inside-out transformational approach to culture change. That is, individuals must change before the team, department, division, and organization can change. After a couple of facilitated workshop sessions, Robert decided he wanted to broaden the exposure to this methodology, and he lined up another fifty senior executives to go through the process.

I ended up in the second cohort to go through the Senn Delaney workshop, and I, like many of my colleagues, was skeptical. I believe almost every executive at UHG was surprised when we heard our CEO hosted an initial culture workshop for his direct reports, along with another top fifteen senior executives. We knew our CEO as a brilliant strategist and world-class accountant, but few of us thought of him as having a bent for culture. We had been conditioned to think the only way to succeed at UHG was to work extremely hard and to be financially astute. We were heavy on the IQ and light on the EQ (emotional quotient), and all the incentives were weighted accordingly.

Many pieces came together quickly through 2010 as our CEO intentionally placed his bet on corporate culture. We formed a Culture Leadership Team (CLT) with leaders from the three cohorts who had been through the culture workshops with a charter aimed at leading the enterprise through a culture transformation. The CLT would be sponsored by the two CEOs leading the two UHG business units, as Robert was clear that he wanted the business to "own" its culture.

As the Chief Administrative Officer for Optum, and a direct report to the Optum CEO, I was asked to facilitate the CLT in its first endeavor: refining our mission and revamping our core values.

Once that task was completed, we shared the results with the original seventy-seven senior executives who had been through the first three culture workshops. No changes to the new mission or core values were suggested, so we then launched Culture Action Teams (CATs) led by CLT members. The objective of these six CATs was to embed the mission and core values fully into the key functions and processes. We also worked through plans to train sixteen senior executives to be facilitators for the culture workshops and to line up the next nine hundred executives to go through them.

Here's the memorandum our chief executive used with our most senior leaders to introduce "Our United Culture." The following is a direct quote from the 2010 brochure we later distributed broadly across the enterprise.

> *We have come to understand that what we hope to achieve as an enterprise and how we collectively approach our endeavors is fundamentally shaped by who we are—what we believe—what we value—how we behave—the sum total of our character as an institution of people—Our United Culture.*
>
> *Culture represents the socially transmitted beliefs, values, and behaviors of our people as a whole. Beliefs, values, and behaviors determine how successful our efforts will be in achieving, improving, and sustaining our performance against our stated goals.*
>
> *We have been too passive over our history in defining, shaping, and protecting the culture we desire—the culture we believe will advance and sustain our full potential as an enterprise. This document represents a first-generation effort to explicitly set forth our institutional character—*

Our United Culture; the beliefs, values, and behaviors we believe will be successful for the enterprise we aspire to be.

Over the next several months, we will set forth how we will measure those values and behaviors and how they are being honored—and what we will do in instances where we understand those beliefs are being compromised.

This is important. We have come to realize that lapses in our culture have caused us to fall short of achieving our full potential as an enterprise. Breakdowns and conflicts in values and behaviors tear at the spirit of our people and cause confusion and lack of clarity over the true nature of our belief and value system. As we move forward into a more challenging and expanding role serving the healthcare needs of society, we need to become clear and aligned on our core beliefs, values, and behaviors—our culture for long-term success.

As we consider the subject of an enterprise culture, we need to put it in the context of our overall purpose as an enterprise. Our stated mission to 'help people live healthier lives' gives strong purpose to our enterprise:

- *in its core focus on helping people*
- *on its positive emphasis—on an ever healthier and productive state*
- *on its emphasis and celebration of life*

But it is an amorphous purpose. Our right to enroll in that purpose must be made clear. We believe our actual role in that mission is to 'make healthcare work for everyone.' And I believe that our collective leadership will guide the way forward.

—Robert, June 10, 2010 (See appendix 1 for entire brochure)

Despite UnitedHealth Group's historically impressive financial performance, our CEO's introductory letter for our core values never mentioned any financial targets. He saw financial and operational performance growth as both a natural expectation of our stronger foundation and as the only true metric of whether Our United Culture was working or not.

He never asked us for a culture index or specific measurement of culture. He didn't want a default defense for the culture work in which we invested. He simply wanted better results, and he was willing to *place his bet* on the logic that with a stronger corporate culture, he would get stronger financial and operational results.

A palpable energy started to form. Difficult to put a finger on it or describe, but people started behaving differently. Sometimes it was dramatic, and sometimes nuanced, but the focus on the individual transformation through the culture workshops, along with multiple approaches to embed our mission and core values into our businesses, started to pay off in multiple ways.

Over the next couple of years, we saw our operational processes and functions change as a direct result of the CAT work.

First, using a core values lens to systemically filter change caused ripple-effect changes into conducting business in a different way.

Second, we saw some people leave the organization who no longer saw themselves "fitting" with the new direction Our United Culture was heading.

Third, we saw all of our key performance indicators (KPIs) continue to improve, despite our taking additional time to engineer performance improvements.

Most importantly for our CEO, he started to hear from our external constituents that something was different. The "feel" of working with us was changing for members, customers, vendors, and strategic partners.

So, did our CEO's bet pay off to invest in corporate culture? Four years after we began our culture journey, a May 6, 2013, *Fortune* magazine interview with our CEO publicly highlighted these results.

> *By financial and market metrics, the company's long-term performance has been nothing short of remarkable. Since going public in 1984 with a mere $7 million in sales, the insurer has delivered annualized returns of 24.7% over the 28-year period to the end of 2012. That's a total return of 48,664%.*
>
> *Only two publicly traded companies did better in that span, drugmaker Amgen (No. 162 in the Fortune 500) and oil refiner HollyFrontier (No. 143). UnitedHealth joined the Fortune 500 in 1995, the first year the list included service companies, and hence its first year of eligibility. That year its sales were $3.8 billion, and it ranked 303rd. This year, at No. 17, it registered sales of $110.6 billion. Its 286-spot rise is one of the most remarkable ascents in the 500's history.*

Our CEO also acknowledged, "We're in the most sensitive area of human endeavor, and we were not respectful of the importance of our role. We're a young company, and we were too self-centered and needlessly aggressive. I'm not proud that we needed to change, but we did."[1]

The numbers speak for themselves, but I'm hopeful you also picked up on a few of the nuanced areas referred to that changed as part of Our United Culture work, such as compassion, relationships, maturity, and humility.

Our CEO placed a big bet on culture. And the positive results continued. In the chart below, you'll see a quick extract of some KPIs for the nine years of the culture journey where I served as the SVP, Culture.

Results	2009	2018
Employee Engagement	72%	83%
Revenue	$87B	$226B
Annual EPS	$3.24	$12.19
Employees	140k	300k
Stock Price	$26	$239

This quick comparison illustrates a statement made by Dr. John Kotter, a professor at the Harvard Business School, "Corporate cultures have a significant impact on firms' long-term economic performance . . . firms where leaders focused on their culture outperformed firms that did not, by a huge margin."[2]

"Culture eats strategy for breakfast" is a quote attributed to Peter Drucker and made famous by Mark Fields, former Ford CEO. Many articles and books have been written to outline why this statement is true, what to do, and how to do it.

Yet, while most people would intellectually assent to its truth, how many times do you hear about a company that set out to intentionally change its culture to get better results?

And of those, how many stuck with it over a long period of time and saw business results make it worth the challenge to continue the change? In fact, a Deloitte 2016 study showed that "nine out of ten executives surveyed believe culture and engagement is important or very important," yet "only 12 percent of companies believe they understand culture."[3]

Throughout each of the next trail markers, you'll see insights gained and lessons learned from our journey. I trust you'll find it useful for yours.

Questions To Consider

1. What is one element shared that you could immediately leverage in your "why" for working on your organization's corporate culture?
2. What stood out to you the most amidst this introductory story about the start of UHG's culture journey? Why is that?
3. What do you think is missing from what you've seen so far that you'll be looking for in the upcoming chapters? Be as specific as you can be here.

Trail Marker #2

Numbers Don't Lie. There Ain't No Culture ROI.

"We believe numbers don't lie, especially when interpreted advantageously."
Chris Wildt

Okay, we've jumped right into talking about placing bets on culture, and now we will get into my claim that you can't calculate a return on investment (ROI) on culture, but we haven't yet defined exactly what we're talking about when we refer to corporate/company/organizational/workplace culture.

To begin, let's remember that the word culture comes from the Latin *cultus*, which means "care," and from the French word *colere*, which means "to till," as in "till the ground." The etymology of this word originates from an agricultural beginning, out of which came "cultivate."

Most of us would recognize that to raise a crop takes constant attention. Watering just once doesn't cut it. The ground must remain moist, not too wet, and not too dry. Weeding once doesn't cut it either. The ground must be periodically weeded to allow roots to deepen and strengthen. You will also need fertilizer or compost to help add nutrients to the soil to make it healthier.

Corporate *culture* must also be fed, tended, watered, and cultivated.

An individual's character is no different. Constant attention must be given to nurture and grow our character, who we are.

Results are *not* quick and easy with either word. The steps to get there may appear simple, but they're not easy (think weeding or watering).

So, with that grounding (no pun intended), back to our definitions for culture. Many definitions exist, but here are some formal and informal ones I like:

- The culture of a company is like the character of an individual (Simon Sinek)[4]
- Culture is the deeper level of basic assumptions and beliefs that are shared by members of an organization, that operate unconsciously and define in a basic "taken for granted" fashion an organization's view of itself and its environment (Edgar Schein)[5]
- The how and why things get done in an organization (CultureIQ)[6]
- A pattern of behavior that is encouraged or discouraged by people and systems over time (Human Synergistics)[7]
- Just the way we do things around here
- Unwritten norms of the organization
- The way you behave when no one is looking

And of course, we have some one-word snapshots many people use to equate to culture: values, spirit, ethos, personality, DNA, and soul.

Let's also lay out why culture is so important. Much research literature exists substantiating a long list of business results directly correlated to a healthy culture. Bottom line profits, net promoter scores, employee engagement, and employee turnover all improve with a healthier corporate culture.

Forbes magazine has stated, "Strong culture results in a 4x increase in revenue growth. An influential culture can account for up to 50 percent of the differential in performance between organizations in the same sector."[8]

Consulting firm Bain & Company has reported that an engaged employee is 44 percent more productive than a satisfied one, but an employee who feels inspired at work is even more productive: nearly 125 percent more productive than a satisfied one.[9]

Tim Cook, Apple CEO, believes very strongly in his company culture. "Apple has a culture of excellence that is, I think, so unique and so special, I'm not going to witness or permit the change of it."[10]

Legendary IBM CEO Louis Gerstner said, "Until I came to IBM, I probably would have told you that culture was just one among several important elements in any organization's makeup and success—along with vision, strategy, marketing, financials, and the like. I came to see, in my time at IBM, that culture isn't just one aspect of the game, it is the game. In the end, an organization is nothing more than the collective capacity of its people to create value."[11]

Based on what you've read so far, and your previous experience, I'm hopeful you can agree with a few key assertions regarding why workplace culture is important:

- Definitionally, people have many choices with both what and how to define workplace culture.

- Mathematically, it's impossible to *calculate* a direct return on investment for workplace culture.

- Many surveys exist that claim to either correlate or causally show that an investment in workplace culture can demonstrate meaningful results, and I would wholly support utilizing those tools and resources.

- Many notable people and institutions have invested significant time and resources to work on and influence their workplace culture.

Now I'd like you to go out on a bit of a limb with me and allow yourself to leave the accounting/operational efficiency side of your brain. I'm not suggesting you leave logic behind, but I am suggesting you allow yourself to simply reflect on your experiences in the workforce, just as an employee tasked with specific steps to follow in your job, and then also in your current role as a workplace leader.

- Think about a definition of workplace culture that works for you and write it down (yep, you can use one from the previous page if you like).

- Think about (and write down) which results emerging from a positive/negative workplace culture could apply to you and your organization.

- Which of those "proof points" resonate with you—which ones would you feel comfortable using to defend your investment of time and resources to improve your workplace culture?

- Now, put your pen down and think about what impacts and influences your culture the most. Think about recollections from your first job. Your worst job. Your best job.

If you're like most people reflecting on those experiences, you'll probably think of a few names and faces with whom you worked. Yes, the nature of the work, the environment, the processes, and products all had an impact, but most of the time, in talking with thousands of people about their recollections, the people with whom they worked had the biggest impact on their experience.

Along with your answers to those four questions, I'd suggest adding intangibles to your logic.

- How do you factor in how you and others make people feel?
- What impact does their belief system bring into the equation?
- Since we're human beings with a *huge* set of biases shaped by our experiences and learnings, how do you factor in a person's "whole self" with all the math and operational processes you can muster?

We can all probably acknowledge that workplace culture is driven and shaped by people, and all of us as human beings bring strengths and weaknesses to the workplace every day. Can we also further acknowledge that no program or process can "fix" every scenario each of us brings to the table, whether baggage or benefits?

Thus, I would ask that you park your mathematical/efficiencies yearnings at the door and allow yourself to believe that investing in workplace culture is worth time, effort, and resources. Furthermore, the benefits of reading further may trigger a specific action step on your part, or it may create an angst that allows you to marinate until you are prompted to take action.

A focus on your workplace's core values ultimately comes down to whether you, as the leader of a team of human beings, choose to relate to your employees as human beings or as fungible commodities functioning more like widgets. How you view those people will become apparent to them (and you) and should shape and refine your answers to those four questions.

Let's assume, for the sake of discussion, that love is one of your core values you want your workplace to use to guide decision-making and behaviors. How would you create an ROI for love?

- Would you create a spreadsheet with macros to figure things out?
- Can you simply tell people to love and move on with their lives?
- Do you just recite a creed about love every morning?
- What do you expect in return for people loving others as part of your core values?
- Do you expect good or bad outcomes?
- If you had a "lens" of love acting as a filter for all of your core operational processes, what would change in them?

Perhaps you don't like love as an example. How about innovation, inclusion, integrity, caring, or excellence? All of these are common core values of organizations with many different definitions. Can they truly provide outcomes beyond their definitions? I submit that they can and do. *But,* only when an investment in them occurs, to make them more meaningful and widespread than an initial marketing campaign to promote them.

They are far more than a rallying cry. More than a branding blitz. More than words in posters and binders. They need to be leveraged into everything an organization is about, starting with individual adoption by every human within that organization.

I have worked with many people in my career at Arthur Andersen and UnitedHealth Group who "get it" and a large number who don't. Ultimately, they voted with their feet and their decision processes. Sure, we all make mistakes, but those who get it recognized/acknowledged mistakes, tried to fix them, apologized, and moved forward, having learned from those mistakes. People who didn't get it either didn't care or understand how to factor in the reality that their employees are people.

Human beings need to believe they are contributing to something bigger than completing their daily tasks. People want to understand why they're doing what they're doing and that it makes a difference. People can't be turned into rigid, mechanical, black and white:

- Plans
- Platforms
- Programs
- Policies
- Processes
- Projects

I call these the 6Ps. Sure, we should utilize those 6Ps to improve production capabilities, but reducing our equations to think people only operate linearly is not only crazy, it's foolish.

The core values I saw defined, displayed, deployed, and demonstrated made a difference in people's lives at the two organizations for which I worked. Those people did their jobs far better than before. Their faith in the organization made them better human beings—better workers, better colleagues, and better problem solvers.

The result? Andersen and UHG got far more out of people than if they had a calculation to mathematically prove out culture, and many people I worked with would testify to that fact as clearly as they would say 2+2=4. Or, as my buddy Bob, who's a quantum physics expert, would say, "Well, maybe not so fast on that 2+2=4 assertion."

I'm not saying we don't want to measure what we treasure. I'm simply saying all that matters can't be measured. Spirit, alignment, clarity, unity, ethos, hope, energy, trust, motivation, inspiration, instinct, and integrity are words with meanings that can't be directly measured, but we all intuitively know they matter.

I've been a student of and practitioner of change management for decades. I've read books, been to seminars, collaborated with teams, and spoken with experts. No one has ever been able to show me a direct calculation for change management.

I can't show you a mathematical ROI on change management, but I can show you train wreck after train wreck from those projects that didn't incorporate those important change management principles.

Forbes further reinforces this view with, "Excellent company culture increases employee retention and can even motivate workers in a way nothing else can. But measuring the impact of company culture on a business's production can be difficult because of how intangible it is. There's no robust methodology for equating benefits from positive company culture to return on investment (ROI)."[12]

At some point, a leader needs to take a step of faith and place their bets with people's time, efforts, and resources, trusting that the outcomes will take care of themselves. Measure what matters, and know not everything that matters can be measured.

In 2013, at our Culture Ambassador Summit, our CEO captured this approach well:

> *"I don't consider Our United Culture an initiative or program. It is a fundamental movement within our enterprise to set the right direction for our character, our thinking, and our behaviors, internally and externally.*
>
> *"I can trace back every significant accomplishment we have achieved to one or more of our cultural values. And, where we have failed, I can trace back each of those events to a critical cultural shortcoming. It is not hard to see that direct line of sight. Try it yourself."*[13]

Questions To Consider

1. Do you agree with the assertion that no ROI calculation exists for corporate culture? Why or why not?
2. Think about a change management initiative in which you've been a part. Could you have mathematically forecasted the impact of the steps you took to ensure success? How did you decide to measure whether the change initiative was successful?

Trail Marker #3

Organizations Are People?

"The purpose of the organization is to enable common men to do uncommon things."
PETER DRUCKER

Corporate culture is not just about the way people behave at work; it's about who they are as people. The individual core values constructing their character will overflow or leak out to others in their normal day-to-day activities.

Corporate culture isn't asking someone to prepare a show of behaviors or to simply comply with directives from a culture office. It is to live out their personal core values through the organization in a way that leads toward a healthy, high-performance organization, versus the dysfunctional, dystopian command and control environment evidenced by so many organizations.

So, with what we've covered so far, let's see if we can agree on several premises:

- Organizational culture is, by logic and definition, unique. An organization is made up of people—the "organisms" that comprise the organization. Each person is uniquely different, and those differences contain the ingredients, the DNA, that your organization will mix together to create either an outstanding or distasteful recipe.
- You, as a senior executive or team leader, can't stop the ingredients from mixing. They absolutely will interact in some fashion. But you can dramatically influence the outcome by recognizing some precepts enabling you to shape the culture you want. Culture is "in there," and it *will* come out. But will it come out in the positive way you desire?
- How can your people "re-present" your organization in the way you would want them to every day, in every situation they encounter?
- You want consistency, but not at the expense of creativity.
- You want trust, but that only happens if people are trustworthy.
- You want innovation, but not at the expense of integrity being compromised.
- You want compassion, but not forsaking profitability.

Challenge: People need to understand how to shape culture.

Result: If they do, they can get better results, feel more fulfilled, and ensure they stay true to the soul of their organization.

So, with those solid foundational reasons, you'd think almost every organization in the world would pay significant attention to its culture.

They would want to understand the ins and outs, the ups and downs, and all arounds of how so many factors influence their culture.

However, if you're like me, most of our experience has been with organizations that don't prioritize culture. For some reason, leaders believe it's either a self-governing fluid dynamic or it's something they simply cannot control or influence, and thus it's not worth their time.

Even if I'm a selfish jerk, I'd want a good culture to bring out the best in people. I want people to do their best work to get better results, and if I can get that with some simple changes to my behavior and work environment, then let's do it!

One could make rational arguments that forcing people to attend a workshop, webinar, or training simply becomes a compliance exercise. A check-the-box affair is absolutely what you *don't* want to occur. Yet if there's not an expectation set by leadership of what they want people in their organization to align around, everyone will have an opinion, and you'll end up with a spaghetti mess.

As attributed to Yogi Berra, he said, "If you don't know where you are going, you might end up someplace else."[14]

Whether workplace culture is, as Louis Gerstner puts it, the "game," a specific business strategy, a team goal, or your overall mission, misalignment causes significant inefficiencies and frustrations.

At this point, we've covered a variety of reasons why culture should matter to an organization. However, let's also consider why it could matter personally to individuals, leading to a different kind of result.

My story begins on a typical Saturday afternoon at four o'clock in the Sparkman household. With our three youngest children now being teenagers involved in many different activities, my wife, Carrie, asked me what everyone's status was for supper that evening.

I had no idea, so I quickly sent out a text. One child answered affirmatively, and I forgot about further follow-up. About five o'clock, Carrie asked again. Now irritated since I didn't have a good answer for her, I sent out another text to the kids, this one a bit sterner than before—I needed an answer. One more child responded, so now I accounted for two of the three.

Becca, our third child, age sixteen, had not responded. After ten minutes, I sent another text. Ten minutes later, I called her and rolled into voicemail. At this point, I was frustrated. Six o'clock hits, and it's now supper time. I still don't have any answers about Becca, and the other kids haven't heard anything either. We have supper together, and the mood is tense. Becca's unusual lack of response hangs over us.

After supper, I ramp up the search efforts. My mood has shifted from frustration to intense concern. I've now texted and called Becca multiple times. I'm now calling her friend's parents, teammates from soccer and basketball, and anyone else we can think of who might know where Becca is. Our minds are filled with anxiety and unspoken fears. This lack of communication from Becca was completely out of character for her.

As nine o'clock arrived, Carrie wanted to engage the police. I kept telling myself there surely was a logical explanation, and I wanted to hold off. As the other kids headed to bed that evening, the tension in our house was palpable. Taylor and Austin shared our growing concerns about their sister's well-being.

Ten o'clock came and went, no Becca. Eleven o'clock slipped by—no Becca. Midnight approached, and I gathered some hope, as that time was our standard curfew. Unless the kids got specific approval from Carrie or me, they were all supposed to be home by midnight. I also had mentally put midnight as a threshold to call the police.

I didn't want to go upstairs to talk with Carrie, knowing it would only compound our fear and frustration with the current circumstances. I also procrastinated calling the police, as I wasn't sure what to say without sounding desperate.

At 12:27 a.m. I heard the external garage door opening. Only our family knew the garage code, so I knew it had to be Becca! My mood shot up from fear and dejection to elation, then plummeted immediately to anger.

The story I had rehearsed on what I would tell her if she were OK immediately took the forefront of my mind. I primed myself to unload on her for all the undue concerns and stress she had put our family through. I was ready.

She could not sneak into her room, as my office was right beside the interior garage door. I heard the door open and shut as her footsteps approached through the hallway to my office. At that split second, I had an epiphany.

Based on the culture workshop experience I had been through, would I act when I knew my mood was not positive, or would I defer to when I would be thinking more clearly and fairly? Was I at my best?

I love my children dearly, and for any of you who have had a sixteen-year-old daughter, you know communication between parent and child is ripe with possibilities of going sideways quickly. At that split second, I remembered I needed to be curious, not angry or judgmental.

Becca burst into the office full of energy and youth. Her look of happiness completely disappeared, however, as she saw the grave look I must have had on my face.

With all of the restraint I could muster, I managed to get out the words "Becca, I am *curious* where you have been, and why you are coming home so late?"

Her face lit up as she eagerly responded—of course, she knew where she had been and why she was late.

"Daddy, I was over at Rachel's house. You remember she's the sister of one of the teammates I had a few years ago, and we were watching a movie."

"Becca," I replied, "why didn't you respond to my voicemails or text messages? We were worried sick about you."

Her face lit up once again, as she had a wonderful answer to this question. "Well, Daddy, my phone battery died, so I couldn't get any voicemails or text messages."

(Mental note: Share with her how she could have borrowed a friend's phone, recharged the battery, or, perish the thought, used a land line. *But*, I didn't say this out loud.)

I dutifully returned to the question at hand. "Becca, why weren't you home on time? You know our curfew is midnight, and you hadn't gotten permission to be out past this time."

For the third time, her face brightened up. "Well, I was going to be home on time, but then Sally needed a ride home, and since Sally's mom was already in bed, I decided to give her a ride home. Her house is on the other side of town, so I had to go out of my way to get her home, and that made me late, so here I am."

At this point, my relief and my growing shame prompted me to give up this interrogation. After all, other than being irresponsible, she was safe, and she had been thoughtful about helping her friend get home.

I quietly said, "OK, Becca, thank you and good night."

I went upstairs and shared with Carrie the good news of Becca getting home. We both agreed we would not let go of the conversation but would follow up in the morning with good accountability reminders.

What's the point of the story? If I had not gone to the organizational culture workshop where I was introduced to the Mood Elevator model (enabling one to think more clearly about one's emotions), I would not have had that insight to avoid emotionally unloading on my sixteen-year-old daughter.

I can't say I've always been adept at catching myself with anger toward my children as they went through their teenage years, but as I write this story, I am grateful all four of our young adult children still appear to enjoy being around Carrie and me. And while I can't causally link most of our behaviors to that outcome with our children, I can unequivocally say the Mood Elevator taught me a huge lesson contributing to that outcome.

Your culture matters. And yet, all that matters can't be measured.

Stronger tangible business results await. Lasting results every human being desires and can experience await as well. Let's see how you can get those results.

Questions To Consider

1. All organizations have cultures. The only choice is whether it shapes you, or you shape it. What do you think of this statement? Perhaps share it with your team and consider their responses as you clarify your "why."

2. Who immediately comes to mind in your organization that reflects your organizational values? Who doesn't seem to reflect those values? Who will influence the others the most?

3. Do you believe people can compartmentalize who they are between home and work? Why or why not? Which is a healthier approach?

Trail Marker #4

Think Framework, Not Formula

"Beware of geeks bearing formulas."
WARREN BUFFETT

Our CEO, Robert, decided to utilize Senn Delaney to initiate our culture transformation process after a conversation with Larry Senn, Senn Delaney's CEO.

After Larry pointed out that no strategy or structure could be effective without a strong cultural foundation, Robert signed off on an initial arrangement letter to begin work with Senn Delaney.

Before attending a two-day workshop facilitated by Senn Delaney, participants were given a book titled *Winning Teams, Winning Cultures* by Larry Senn and Jim Hart, where we learned that we would go through the DURAM culture-shaping model. DURAM is an acronym for:

- Diagnose the existing culture and business needs and *define* the desired culture.

- *Unfreeze* the old dysfunctional behaviors and connect people to the new desired behaviors through insight-based training.
- *Reinforce* the new behaviors by aligning all HR systems and providing ongoing reinforcement for all individuals.
- *Apply* the new behaviors to improve business results.
- *Measure* progress for individuals, teams, and the organization.[15]

This approach resonated with many of us because the model paralleled a six-sigma model most were familiar with called DMAIC (Define, Measure, Analyze, Improve, and Control). With the topic of culture being seen as an ambiguous one approached by a company full of people aimed at supporting evidence-based medical decisions, having a structured view of tackling it appealed to us as well.

Ultimately, the key to Senn Delaney's methodology working was the inside-out versus outside-in view of individual change they introduced us to via the culture-shaping workshop. Preaching culture broadly or trying to teach people individually wouldn't create a cultural change. Allowing individuals to experience something and then *convince themselves* there is a better way to approach life, changing from the inside out, is critical to lasting change.

Since culture is inevitably changed one day, one person at a time, and there are constant opportunities to shape it (or it shapes you), then the causal need for individual behavior change is critically important. The individual has to arrive at the decision to change themselves.

Carl Rogers, one of the founders of humanistic psychology, said, "The only learning which significantly influences behavior is self-discovered, self-appropriated learning," and that "such self-discovered learning truth that has been personally appropriated and assimilated in experience, cannot be directly communicated to another."[16]

Basically, he contends that all humans have a desire to learn, and the failure to learn and change stems from the learning environment/situation, not the person's inability to learn.

A person's character can reflect the environment from which they learn. Our character is constantly in motion, being affected by thousands of thoughts, decisions, and actions we make every day.

As a parent of four children, I've watched stages of their character evolve:

- When the kids were three years old, did they share with others?
- When the kids were fifteen, were they good teammates?
- When they turned twenty-one, how responsible were their individual decisions and actions?
- As thirtysomethings, how are they contributing to/serving others?

The older they became, the clearer their character became.

I can't point to any specific formula, model, recipe, or set of instructions that produced their character. My wife and I had thousands of interactions with our children on all levels of communication. To pick out any specific instance or area that pinpointed changes in their character along the way is impossible. All I can point to are foundational family values and principles we tried to teach and reinforce as they grew.

A corporate culture journey is similar. Thousands of things can impact your culture. But if you are grounded upon a foundation of core values, with a framework allowing for flexibility with how you approach situations, then you can teach and reinforce it along the way.

Culture-shaping is best done through a framework, not a formula.

Early in our culture transformation journey, our senior leadership team (SLT) at Optum Health (one of the six operational segments of UnitedHealth Group) saw the framework deliver results at our inaugural Service Heroes program. Leveraging what we saw working at UnitedHealthcare, we launched a program to recognize operational employees for their everyday great service.

We gathered nominations throughout the year, with the criteria shaped from our core values, and then our SLT selected one hundred employees to participate in an all-expenses-paid trip to San Diego.

The two-day trip included their spouse/significant other, a fair amount of leisure time, learning activities, breakout time with our leaders, and a formal recognition dinner for their collective achievements.

A key element of the event was that our nine-person SLT hosted the event. We were dedicated to serving the two hundred people however we could, from welcoming them as they entered the hotel and helping with their bags to intentionally being available in common areas for casual interaction throughout the event.

As we closed out the last morning's activities with remarks by our COO, I followed to administratively wrap up the event before turning everyone loose for leisure time in the afternoon. One of the Houston attendees, Nancy, raised her hand—I had to recognize her. She stood up, took the microphone, and said she wanted to thank our SLT on behalf of all the attendees. She commented on several of the activities and the location, and then she emphasized how much they especially appreciated spending time with our SLT. As she ended her comments, the entire room stood to give us a standing ovation. I was emotionally moved and don't remember how I closed out after that or got off the stage. Our entire SLT was similarly overwhelmed!

As I've reflected on what may have triggered their heartfelt appreciation to us, I'm convinced many small things culminated in how they felt about our SLT and the event. Not any one remark or behavior generated that reaction. We had good food, a beautiful environment, activities focused on Our United Culture, but ultimately, I believe our SLT walking our talk around our values of compassion and relationships is reflected in words attributed to Maya Angelou:

"People will never forget how you made them feel."[17]

I can't remember most of what we did that weekend in San Diego, but I'll never forget that moment.

And what's the metric for that? The calculation? The formula? The infamous KPI?

Ah, but the *value! Huge* value. And no singular way to measure it!

How Will You Measure Your Life, by Clayton Christensen, was an early influencer on our approach to culture. In fact, we began distributing the July 2010 Harvard Business Review article he authored to all of our culture workshop attendees. I appreciated his perspective that most of what we work for gives us quick feedback on whether we're being successful. He points out, however, that this immediate gratification does not truly measure your life's contributions.

Like life, there's no formula for culture. This is one reason many leaders can't quite get their arms around it. It's not a linear model. Yes, you can have DURAM as a framework, but an organization is a living and breathing entity filled with humans constantly influenced by whatever hits them. We have to embrace life happening with an EQ, rarely knowing the outcome. We must have faith; one definition of faith that gives me a chuckle states, "Faith begins precisely where thinking leaves off."[18]

At many points in our culture journey, I learned to put things in motion for our employees without knowing where they would go. In fact, most of what we did through the culture office was exactly that.

Faith takes risks and exposes vulnerability—that reflects authenticity, because that's real life. Rarely do we know what outcomes will result, but if you try to control culture, think that it's formulaic, think that A+B=C, then you'll miss opportunities for your organization or team. If you're encountering culture as "that is just the way things work around here," then bingo! That's a prime opportunity for change.

Transaction versus transformation is much more than changing a few letters in the words.

Some leaders believe that if they do enough transactions, they'll get transformation. Kind of a "fake it till you make it" approach. Nothing could be further from the truth.

Changing corporate culture isn't just change management on steroids.

Change is simply a new way of *doing*. Transformation is a new way of *being*.

Changing corporate culture is more than going through the motions on a set of behaviors—that is, compliance. It's broader, although behaviors are important in the equation. Ultimately, if you don't change behaviors, you end up with hypocrisy. But while tasks can be monitored and people held accountable for completion, the "how" is much more difficult to track. Behaviors can flip on a dime—in a nanosecond. Most of us can recall a Dr. Jekyll and Mr. Hyde in our work history.

We behave the way we behave for a reason. It makes sense to us.

But what if there were actually a better way of doing something? For many objective, measurable outcomes, we can easily agree that something is true; however, for our personal behaviors in an ongoing pattern of unique situations, it's very easy to tell ourselves that our behavior is correct, warranted, or necessary.

Of course, the reason is simple—we believe we're right and/or the situation "called for" that behavior. Or we "responded as appropriate," so we very seldom do a post-mortem on our personal behavior.

Thus, we don't change, and those behaviors become ingrained into our style/personality/mode of operation. In essence, they start to define who we are.

Many times, leaders learn what their culture is (versus what is advertised) through situations they never would have planned, and unfortunately, not often in a good way.

Remember a few years ago with United Airlines, when an airline attendant attempted to drag a customer off a plane? Hmmm, I'd never think to put a warning against such behavior in an operations manual. Consider Volkswagen, which has had flaws in its cars. Wells Fargo with fake accounts. All these serious downfalls point to "culture" as a culprit.

OK, so even if we could agree that these corporations' issues were due to culture, what can you or should you do about it?

On one level, whether you view transforming culture as a superlative state of nirvana to pursue the nobleness and egalitarianism of organizational success,

or,

as a necessary topic to address because "it" seems to be getting in the way of what you believe your brilliant business strategy to be.

Culture still deserves and needs your attention!

Questions To Consider

1. How do you believe a person's character is formed? How can an organization influence that?

2. Have you worked with other business approaches that leveraged frameworks rather than formulas? How well did that work? What similarities or differences exist with corporate culture?

3. What do you think of the statement, "Transaction versus transformation is much more than changing a few letters in the words"? Do you agree or disagree, and why?

4. With whatever headline workplace culture failure you've read about or comes to mind, could the shortfall have been formulaically addressed?

Trail Marker #5

Lousy Music Equals Lousy Culture

"The only music I don't like is bad music."
QUINCY JONES

"There are more bad musicians than there is bad music."
ISAAC STERN

If I asked you to think about your favorite song, would your choice be based on the music or the words? If you're like most people, the music in the melody holds sway by a wide margin over the words. In fact, many people have a favorite song and don't even know the words.

Or think about a musical theme to a movie or television sitcom you like: perhaps *Star Wars, The Office, Cheers, MASH*, or *Friends*? If you're familiar with any of those shows, odds are high you can hum the tune. The simple arrangement of a few notes creates a lasting melody that almost everyone can appreciate.

Our pastor once stated, "Lame words set to great music equals a great song. Great words set to lame music equals a lame song."[19]

He then equated musical notes to how we live our lives. If we have great words, but our actions aren't winsome and loving, then as 1 Corinthians 13:1 states, "If I could speak all the languages of earth and of angels, but didn't love others, I would only be a noisy gong or a clanging cymbal."[20] Noise, not music.

On one level, music composition appears rather simple. There are eight notes to an octave, before going up or down the register to the next octave. On a piano, there are eighty-eight keys one could use to compose music. But when you put in elements of music theory such as melody, harmony, rhythm, tempo, meter, and key, along with a wide variety of musical instruments available to perform the music, the combinations allow people to continue to create original musical scores for hundreds of years.

America's Got Talent has had some amazing performances, many times of popular songs. On one occasion, Simon Cowell, one of the judges, stopped the contestant singing after she had sung for only ten seconds. He told her he didn't like the song she was singing and asked if she could sing something else.

She replied that she could, and she then proceeded to wow both him and the audience. He later explained that her first song just didn't seem to arouse the passion he thought should be in her as she performed it. The second song did the trick!

What lasts isn't just in the musical score or the words but also in how it is performed. As an illustration, listen to "The Sound of Silence" performed by Simon & Garfunkel and then compare it to the same song's performance by Disturbed or Pentatonix. I guarantee you'll be moved in different ways.

My good friend and author of the book *Good to the Core*, John Blumberg, shared, "*Values are to your core like notes are to music. Together they create the melody that inspires others to sing a new song.*"[21]

Allow a moment for your mind to wrap around that.

Everyone has access to the same musical notes to create a memorable song. But we can't all do that.

We all have access to the same words to create memorable core values. But we don't all do that.

If you work in an organization with core values, you have an opportunity to make them come alive. Will *you* do that?

Your musical notes and score may be different, but I'm sure it won't be "Chopsticks." I'm hopeful you'll pick up a few orchestral maneuvers from this book to use in your arrangement.

One of my favorite animated movies is *Klaus*, with a theme song called "Invisible." I'd encourage you to play it to capture what I'm trying to communicate here. For me, the melody's lyrics express these themes:

- Many times what means the most to us can't be seen, it can only be felt.
- Initiating those feelings can start with a few steps and create memories that will last forever.
- How you treat others makes the music.

Every corporate culture is unique. Pretending there's a formula to get you there is a disservice to the tremendous, uniquely distinctive culture you can help create. Create one you can *feel*.

While music theory is an important subject filled with truths about making music, not all musical theorists are good musicians.

Case in point.

At UnitedHealth Group, we constantly focus on solving massive problems because we deal with large numbers of people and significant reams of data. To that end, we became accomplished at the 6Ps: plans, platforms, programs, policies, processes, and projects. We relied on the 6Ps because they:

- Had a tangible beginning and an end;
- Could be tightly monitored and controlled;
- Could be reviewed by multiple layers of supervision to spot potential errors;
- Usually had multiple KPIs applied;
- Could easily have accountability assigned; and
- Were linear in nature; formulas generally worked within them.

So of course, despite Senn Delaney introducing us to the DURAM framework for our culture transformation, we initially tried to solve culture through the 6Ps, since that structure had worked well for us in many other areas.

But the science of the theory didn't equate to results. *We realized workplace culture is as much art as it is science.*

We also realized three premises behind this truth:

- Workplace culture is far bigger than any and all of the 6Ps,
- Some of the strengths of the 6Ps actually worked against culture transformation, but
- You will need all the 6Ps, in some way, to enable culture transformation.

Many of the Trail Markers shared in later chapters directly reflect this insight.

Many of our natural instincts we had to "unlearn" to be successful.

Dr. Larry Senn shared with me early on in our culture transformation journey, "Dave, organizations resist what they need most."

For us, the 6Ps proved to be formidable opponents. When we could instill the framework versus formula mentality at the forefront, we then could channel those 6Ps to highly enable Our United Culture. But phew. Some battles were needed!

Just because you don't start with the 6Ps and lean into a framework doesn't mean you don't have rigor and discipline applied to the objective. It's just a looser art form than the science usually expected. Deliberate intentionality is still necessary—it looks different from the 6Ps because many of those impossible-to-measure attributes (unity, energy, spirit, trust) are at the forefront, or the foundation, of the transformation.

You can't think culture will naturally happen in the right way, with the results you believe should manifest. Whatever you leave to chance is just that—chance, and then the things that get done are the transactional tasks rather than the deeper, more insightful, relational, and longer-term transformation that takes time to unfold.

Jim Collins, in *Good to Great*, stated, "In determining the right people, the good-to-great companies placed greater weight on character attributes than on specific educational background, practical skills, specialized knowledge, or work experience."[22]

We found this to be true: *Transformed character transforms culture.*

Questions To Consider

1. Does your organization have a great song? Which is better: the words or the music?

2. Which of the 6Ps in your organization are working? Which might benefit from strengthening through your core values lens?

3. What's a lesson you've learned from a prior organization for which you've worked that has influenced your work on core values or the 6Ps at your current organization?

Trail Marker #6

Words Matter

"Colors fade, temples crumble, empires fall,
but wise words endure."
EDWARD THORNDIKE

Probably the most moving illustration I've seen about the power of words is a short video entitled "The Power of Words," which extracts a story from renowned advertiser David Ogilvy about a blind man begging for money.

The video opens with a blind beggar at the base of some outside stairs of a government building or bank. His cardboard sign has a short message written on it in block letters stating, "I AM BLIND, PLEASE HELP." It is a cold day, and he is bundled up on the steps, hoping people will stop by and drop money in his soup can. Many pass by, but only a few drop coins in his soup can.

A woman approaches in sunglasses and a pea jacket. She initially walks by without dropping any coins in the can, but then she turns around, pulls a Sharpie out of her purse, reaches for his cardboard sign, and on the other side of his sign writes out new words. While she is writing out these new words, he is shown reaching out to feel her shoes to identify her. She then places the sign with the new message against the steps facing the people passing by and leaves. The video does not show us what the words say.

The new words immediately appear to make a difference!! As people walk by, rarely does one walk by without dropping something into the beggar's soup can. Soon his soup can is overflowing with pocket change from these gifts.

At the end of the day, the woman in the peacoat comes back, and she stops to look at the blind man and the soup can full of coins. He reaches out and feels her shoes again, thus recognizing her as the woman who changed his sign.

He asked her, "What did you do to my sign?"

She responded with a smile, "I wrote the same but with different words."

"Thanks, Love," he responded.

She turned to walk away, and as the music played, the camera panned over to show the new words written on the cardboard sign. They stated,

"Today is a beautiful day, and I *can't* see it."

The video ends with two sentences: "Change your words. Change your world."[23]

As you think about the foundation of your organization and the people working within it, keep in mind human beings are amazingly complex individuals, with many filters and many blind spots. Much as a new product has a set of operating instructions in it, hopefully designed to be concise, clear, and direct to put the product together properly, so should a workplace's core values provide the clarity, simplicity, and action through their definition to do so in a scalable manner. This means you don't have to constantly reexplain what you mean. (Although remember, repetition is not redundancy.)

When I was in the corporate travel business, a familiar scenario was used in training travel agents to highlight the need for specificity and clarity in determining where the traveler wanted to go. The standard line, "Are you headed to Portland?" wasn't enough. "Maine or Oregon?" needed to be included for true clarity. Both are well-known destinations, but at different ends of the country.

Yet many organizations have treated their corporate values as simply buzzwords on their websites or corporate posters. The words may be good, but they lack clear definition. Words like *integrity, creativity, innovation, respect*, and *fun* are useful words, but they can have various meanings to different people. Unless time is taken to give specificity and a full definition, clarity will not be achieved. If clarity is not achieved, then everyone will be moving in different directions, and the power of the collective character will not only be chaotic, but diluted and possibly even harmful.

Here's a simple two-by-two grid to illustrate what can happen when clarity is in place with the outcomes that could go with it.

Yes clarity, bad results = **Interpretation**	Yes clarity, good results = **Intentionality**
No clarity, bad results = **Ignorance**	No clarity, good results = **Intuition**

Ignorance. First, when a definition isn't given and bad outcomes occur, we can blame ignorance. "He just didn't know" becomes the standard default position with victim mentality results. For any of you with corporate communications experience, you'll immediately know if there is a lack of communication; people will fill in the blanks, and usually, the message they create is driven toward a negative outcome. People rarely reach positive conclusions about what an organization wants to communicate.

Here's an example. When I say the word *bear* verbally, what do you immediately think of? Most people think of an animal, whether a polar bear, panda bear, or grizzly bear. But if you hadn't seen the word *bear* written out, you may have phonetically heard the word *bare* and arrived at a different meaning. Then again, with either spelling of *bear* or *bare,* you could use them in different ways to use those words and sentences that again have different meanings. For example, you may "bear one another's burdens." Or "the cupboards are bare."

When I've done this exercise in person, many different angles and definitions appear; however, two words/definitions rarely show up. The words Bayer, as in Bayer aspirin, or Behr, as in Behr paint, rarely come into people's minds when they hear the word bear phonetically. If you really want to have fun with this exercise, try throwing southern accents into the word *bahr*, and you'll get, again, a different set of conclusions.

Intuition. Second, when little or no definition is given, but perhaps good results occur, I chalk that up to an individual's intuition, or perhaps even blind luck. We've all heard the adage, "Even a blind squirrel finds a nut." When clarity is not achieved, people can still make good decisions based on their intuition, fueled by their skills, abilities, or core values. For example, they may still be able to assemble a product without good instructions because their intuition leads them to good results.

Interpretation. Third, even with a good definition, bad results can still occur. This could result from an extension of ignorance, but assuming the individual has read and digested the definition, we all still have personal filters at work, causing us to interpret what is defined in different ways. I chalk that up to a lack of good interpretation of what has been said, which is always a possibility, even with well-defined definitions. For example, one of history's most stellar documents, the United States' Constitution, is constantly being interpreted by government officials, politicians, and the general public. Rational, well-intentioned people can arrive at different conclusions based on their interpretation of the core document.

Intentionality. The fourth scenario exists when definitions are clearly outlined and good outcomes are achieved. Intentionality accomplished. We can easily relate when we follow a clear set of instructions that work and don't rely on our intuition. It clears us through our ignorance and closes gaps in our various interpretations. A fine line between scenarios three and four, with the prevailing differentiator being the whole document being used to help interpret new views that develop. In this case, precedent decisions are used to help further define new cases. Thankfully, in workplace-culture situations, many different interpretations, when grounded upon a core, will create even more intentionality with which the organization can act.

We have all probably experienced a situation when exactly the right words are used, which caused us to respond in a positive, inspired fashion. In the historical drama *The Darkest Hour*, the newly appointed Prime Minister Winston Churchill is portrayed as mercurial, doubting, and forceful, all at the same time. Churchill spent time carefully crafting the speeches he shared with parliament and the British people. One great line in the film captures his focus: "He mobilized the English language and sent it into battle."[24]

Whether it was his speech to the House of Commons and what's become known as the "Blood, toil, tears and sweat," speech, or the "We shall never surrender" speech delivered to Parliament, Churchill was an incredible orator, but leading up to that was his depth as an editor. In the original copies of his speech still in existence, all of them are heavily self-edited. Producer/screenwriter Anthony McCartan said, "He was scrupulous about the impact of each word. He preferred short words and the repetition of short words."[25]

Another illustration bringing this point home is the book *Exactly What to Say* by Phil Jones. With over a million books published in the United States each year, only ten of them sell one million copies within twelve months following their release. *Exactly What to Say* is one such book.

I had the opportunity to meet Phil and hear him speak at a leadership conference. On one level, I was amazed to see how simple words and phrases can be used to influence and impact people. Yet on another level, I was not surprised at all because throughout my time at UnitedHealth Group with workplace culture, we constantly found ourselves saying, "*It's simple, just not easy.*"

Questions To Consider

1. Have you ever experienced a situation where the choice of words gave a dramatically different outcome, like the blind beggar story? If so, what was it, and what was the outcome? If not, where could it be applied in your organization?

2. On the two-by-two clarity grid, where do you think your organization lands? How could it be improved?

3. Where have you encountered something "Simple, just not easy"? What was it, and how did you address it?

Trail Marker #7

Improv Has A Place, Just Not Here

"It's important to be precise about words,
because of the thought value of them-they frame
and shape so much of the way we understand things."
MICHAEL NESMITH

I'm hopeful that, at this point, you are finding your head nodding in agreement with the need to specifically define your core values. But you may find yourself asking, "How does this all work? I've seen many organizations with posted core values, and even some with behaviors outlined beside them. Just how specific do the definitions need to be?"

The answer to that question shows up with some of the early developments in the UnitedHealth Group culture journey.

After the first three culture workshops Senn Delaney conducted with our executives, a group of us volunteered to take the next step in their work plan for us to create a UnitedHealth Group cultural statement. The statement aimed to capture what we wanted to achieve in changing the corporate culture. My boss, an EVP who also functioned as our CEO's "consigliere," asked me to facilitate the group of volunteers.

When the eleven volunteers got together to begin this work, within the first thirty minutes, we concluded we did not believe the right answer was to create a cultural statement but to revisit our core values. All of us had read the book *Winning Teams Winning Cultures* and saw in the studies Senn Delaney had done over many years that successful organizations had six essential characteristics in their core values, and if those values were lived out, results improved.

After getting approval from our CEO, we looked at the six segments of UnitedHealth Group and the values articulated for each segment. We saw overlap in many areas, with some using the same words to reflect those values. One of our team members even put together a grid of the six segments' results, along with the Senn Delaney six essential characteristics, so we could see everything on one piece of paper.

We had also received specific instruction that while some of the new core values could be aspirational, some of the core values should reflect attributes that had brought us significant success over the past decade. We didn't want to lose what had gotten us to this point, but we wanted to gain something that would take us beyond our current trajectory.

Six hours into our first meeting, we had drafted the five values to propose for UnitedHealth Group. Over the next couple of months, the draft core values and the brief tagline descriptions barely changed.

The next step was to write paragraphs describing what those five core values and the tag lines meant. Our CEO had been clear with us. He didn't want a few words in a pithy PowerPoint. He used the illustration that if the founders of our country had done that, we would not have lasted as a democracy.

After several drafts of these paragraphs circulated to capture edits among our team, I submitted them to our CEO for his review. A few days later, his feedback came with the construct added of segregating the paragraphs for each value into what we believe, what we value, and how we should behave.

Several more refining edits took place, and then our CEO presented the values and their construct to his senior leadership team. It was endorsed as written.

The next question was how to roll it out to the seventy-seven executives who had been through the first three workshops with Senn Delaney. Since they were grounded in the key concepts, tools, and techniques of the Senn Delaney DURAM process, they would be, by definition, the right initial group to give us feedback and approval on what we would then roll out to our 140,000 employees.

I was charged with putting together a brochure to showcase these five values in a way that was different than how most things were rolled out at UnitedHealth Group. I immediately connected with our Optum Health chief marketing officer to get his creative mind applied to this task. He pulled in his content creator to help us visually construct the brochure.

Executive leadership had characterized this culture effort as "The Way Forward," and after many suggestions on what to call this journey, we landed on "Our United Culture." The Marketing gurus contributed quickly and creatively to develop the brochure into a beautiful fivefold handout, which included the five values and their constructs, along with a description of how we would measure success. It was introduced through the specific letter from our CEO that I shared with you in Trail Marker #1. On the back of the foldout brochure were the names of all seventy-seven leaders who had been through the process so far.

Since I've talked so much about how words matter, I'd suggest taking a minute to go back to read our CEO's brochure letter at the beginning of Trail Marker #1, and the five values and measuring success in appendix 1.

Our CEO was comfortable with the new words describing our values, beliefs, and behaviors, but he also wanted the flexibility to shift if we received meaningful feedback to warrant any changes. So we called this version 1.0, and in the rollout process, we actively engaged with the seventy-seven leaders to see what changes they would suggest. Some suggestions were made, although none were seriously campaigned for, and throughout my time at UnitedHealth Group, not one word changed.

Words matter—our CEO took them seriously. He wanted this undertaking to succeed. In addition to the tangible reasons for his decision to transform culture shared in Trail Marker #1, there is a back story.

When our CEO joined UnitedHealth Group from Arthur Andersen in 1998, he already saw the importance of being clear about how the organization should operate. He created what he called the "Rules of the Road" and passed out a binder outlining the values and policies he wanted to incorporate to the senior leadership team. If you had a chance to read that binder, your head would probably nod in approval of what he articulated. However, as I will discuss in Trail Marker #8, nothing was done to get the senior leadership team to own what he had advanced.

As you may have recognized in the cover letter for the brochure introducing our core values, our CEO took the opportunity to define what culture was to him and associated the "character of the organization" to make culture more tangible to us. He then used the five values to define what UnitedHealth Group's character should be.

Thus began the taxonomy for Our United Culture. A couple of years later, we chose to use the word "principles" for all of the Senn Delaney concepts, tools, and techniques, such as accountability, Be Here Now, energy, and mood elevator. The principles gave further definition about how to live out the values. They weren't just behaviors, but they were the essence of the workshop takeaways that individuals could utilize to transform themselves.

About a year later, we started associating "protocols" with those principles, so people could see even more practically how to live out the principles and values.

For example, to better live out the value of performance, we apply the principle of positive energy being brought to a team. By employing the protocol of standing up on a phone call, physiologically, you will have better energy, which will then contribute to your positive attitude and energy contribution.

So, to summarize, we created this taxonomy for Our United Culture:

- Culture, which is defined as
- Character, which is defined by our
- Values, which are lived out using
- Principles, that are enabled by
- Protocols which are tangible practices anyone can do

Culture is indeed an amorphous topic, as our CEO described in the brochure letter. By having taken the time to specifically define as many avenues as we could, and to arrange a taxonomy to give clear linear connections of beliefs, values, behaviors, and outcomes, we made significant headway in helping people understand how we wanted Our United Culture to work.

Questions To Consider

1. What struck you the most from seeing how the UnitedHealth Group values were born? What could the application be for your organization?

2. How might more clarity through some type of workplace culture taxonomy help you advance your cultural journey?

Trail Marker #8

The Power Of Belief Isn't The Only Thing, But It's A Mighty Thing

"Live your beliefs and you can turn the world around."
HENRY DAVID THOREAU

For an individual to fully take ownership of something, to personally appropriate the words you have created for your purpose, mission, and core values, they need to come to terms with it at the deepest level. The organizational belief system needs to be comprehended and integrated with their belief system.

The power of belief has been shown throughout history to be one of the most powerful forces on the planet. Margaret Thatcher once said, "Europe was created by history. America was created by philosophy."[26] Bono, the lead singer of the Irish band U2, is often credited with saying something similar: "America is not just a country; it is an idea."

But it was G.K. Chesterton who identified the philosophy, the idea to which Thatcher and Bono referred: "America is the only nation in the world that is founded on a creed. That creed is set forth with dogmatic and even theological lucidity in the Declaration of Independence. It is encoded into our (America's) national DNA: 'We hold these truths to be self-evident, that all men are created equal, that they are endowed by their Creator with certain unalienable Rights, that among these are Life, Liberty and the pursuit of Happiness.'"[27]

Outside of America, one can also look at history to see how the Romans and Kublai Khan treated the people they conquered. They allowed them to maintain their belief systems and only exacted payments and taxes from them. Somehow, they knew that to try to wrestle the conquered peoples' belief systems into their own was too difficult.

As a World War II buff, I've been intrigued with the story of how Ford Motor Company's Willow Run assembly plant helped change the outcome of the war, particularly in the European theater. In 1940, President Roosevelt declared the United States needed fifty thousand aircraft to be ready for the growing storm of a global war. America only had three thousand such aircraft at the time. "Roosevelt didn't have faith in the government to get America to a place where it could mobilize effectively. So, he turned to the automotive industry with its efficiencies and understanding of mechanization."[28]

Ford, famous for its mass production of the Model T years before, had no capacity to build such combat aircraft. However, one of their senior leaders, Karl Sorenson, believed it could be done. He backed up that belief with action to capture the vision of Edsel Ford, the forty-five-year-old CEO of Ford, and the board by investing heavily in a plant at Willow Run to win the contract to build the B-24 Liberator bombers. It's a fascinating story how strong belief in their abilities provided the genesis of Ford being able to produce bombers at the rate of one every sixty-three minutes by the middle of the war.

The real obstacles and initial lack of belief were difficult to overcome. For example, the previous company charged with building the aircraft, Consolidated, had invested thousands of hours into plans that yielded poor production and results. The media, upon learning Ford had been given the contract, jokingly reported, "And of course, it was written in the paper, it must be true."[29] In fact, the media referred to the Willow Run assembly plant as the "Will It Run?" plant.

Aside from Mr. Sorensen, no one forecasted Ford's incredible level of productivity. To illustrate, there were fifteen thousand parts in a Ford motor car at the time, and to produce a Liberator bomber, there were 1,150,000 parts per plane. The power of their conviction overrode the power of ordinary logic and rationale, turning it into one of the greatest production stories of all time.

Conviction trumps logic.

In addition to the power of belief reflected in a country's approach and an organization's approaches, many teams and individuals have believed in themselves above what others have said to achieve success beyond what anyone else believed possible.

The 1969 Miracle Mets winning the World Series. George Washington Carver developing over three hundred uses for the peanut. Abraham Lincoln getting elected president after numerous election defeats. Kurt Warner becoming the Super Bowl MVP, while just a few months before, he was stocking grocery store shelves. Many more examples exist.

All organizations can achieve remarkable success, but to do so, they must allow opportunity for people's belief systems to connect with the organization. By developing a noble mission and core values and then enabling people to link their personal beliefs to them, huge results can be gained. 2 + 2 can = 5!

It's a classic reflection of planting a few seeds and reaping a huge harvest. Remember, *culture* is an outgrowth of the same root word as *cultivate*. Much like a crop, soil has to be tilled and fertilized, seeds must be planted, watered, and weeds removed. It is a constant process, not a one-and-done activity.

As you read the different illustrations about the power of belief, you may have concluded that these people not only believed in themselves, but they also had faith in their abilities to fulfill that belief. Bingo! I found myself coming to that same realization as we started seeing many different outcomes take place in both individuals, teams, and departments as people began personally appropriating our core values.

Faith is defined in Merriam-Webster's dictionary as "confidence or trust in a person or thing" and "belief that is not based on proof." *Belief* is defined as "something that is accepted, considered to be true, or held as an opinion."[30]

I certainly found those definitions playing out in our culture journey at UnitedHealth Group. *Belief* accepted our mission and core values. *Faith* took action upon that belief. To describe this, we used the word *transformation*. This is so important. Otherwise, activities are surface-level, check-the-box approaches without getting deeper movement. Unless there's action based on those beliefs, going beyond mere thought, nothing will change.

We found ourselves shifting our thinking, establishing a power of belief, and evolving into faith based upon those core values. What came out of that was, as our CEO called it, a movement.

In October 2011, we gathered about three hundred culture ambassadors (more on them in Trail Marker #11) in Minneapolis to glean what had been accomplished with Our United Culture, celebrate it, and cast a vision for the future. Our CEO, as the owner of Our United Culture, shared a few remarks about where we had been and where he was hoping we could be going by leveraging Our United Culture.

After his brief remarks, he opened the floor for questions. One person asked, "What do you see as the obstacles for Our United Culture to continue to grow within UnitedHealth Group?"

He responded, "I don't believe I could stop this even if I tried. What has begun here is a movement."[31]

I believe it's important to note that the word *movement* was never ascribed to Our United Culture until that moment, about eighteen months *after* we had begun the cultural transformation journey. A movement can be a wonderful goal, but rarely throughout history have we seen movements described as such ahead of time. To do so would be an overreach.

One of the more notable movements in America's history is the Civil Rights Movement led by Dr. Martin Luther King Jr.. In reviewing the history of this movement:

- Dr. King's reflections and experiences influencing his thinking
- Led to his strong beliefs becoming convictions
- Which then turned into faith
- With resulting actions taking him and others far beyond his initial thinking.

The resulting movement transformed America's civil rights.

My father was a pastor for over forty years. A sermon illustration I heard him use many times was about a tightrope walker who claimed he could walk across Niagara Falls. He asked how many people believed he could do it. Almost the entire audience raised their hands. He then walked a tightrope across Niagara Falls and returned to the amazement and celebration of the crowd.

He then asked the crowd, "Who thinks I can walk back across Niagara Falls on the tight rope pushing a wheelbarrow?" The crowd gasped but quickly shifted into cheering him on to accomplish this feat.

Without delay, he rapidly crossed the expanse of the falls again, this time pushing a wheelbarrow. When he arrived on the other side, he asked the crowd another question. "Who thinks I can walk the tightrope across the Falls, again pushing a wheelbarrow, but this time with a person sitting in the wheelbarrow?"

The crowd enthusiastically cheered their support. He then asked, "Who would like to volunteer to sit in the wheelbarrow?"

You could have heard a pin drop.

You see, people intellectually believed he could do it, but they lacked the faith to act upon that belief.

I heard another pastor describe faith with three different stages. I've adjusted the statements to apply these stages to corporate culture:

Head knowledge. Much like I've described in the story above, people who believe culture exists, but it's influenced by bring-your-dog-to-work days, ping-pong tables in the break area, and free food in the cafeteria. They don't think about it much, and they tend not to care much in the collective effort of the organization as much as they care about themselves.

Neck knowledge. This belief system functions as the neck, swiveling the head to pick and choose what they think can work for them, and then applies that belief to others. These people can relate to some of the values and principles and may see the benefit of some individual change. For example, concepts like accountability, clarity, alignment, and innovation make sense to them, and they want to see them emphasized in the company, particularly to affect others' behaviors. However, they primarily want to rely on control and the 6Ps to influence culture.

Heart knowledge. A belief where you put your confidence, trust, and hope in the foundation of your core values. While there are many ingredients in corporate culture, emphasis will stay on the values and principles necessary to shape the 6Ps. These people realize, "I need to change to fit the values. There truly is a better way of being, that's more fulfilling, and gets better results." While the neck offers a jersey to wear, the heart has a story to share.

Once you've given enough thought to the words for your organizational purpose, mission, and core values to be compelling and inspirational, you can then help people personally appropriate those words.

We discovered that when people took ownership of our core values, those values melded into their thinking and transformed into beliefs. Convictions flowed from those beliefs, which led to faith, positive actions, and real results.

Activities we couldn't ever prescribe took place. People were hugely effective because they lived out their culture from their hearts. In fact, when we tried to prescribe things, that's when the tools turned into rules, and we found ourselves evolving in some situations to a legalistic environment versus a vibrant, rich, faith-based life.

An author I've come to admire, C.S. Lewis, makes this comment on faith:

> *"Faith is the art of holding onto things your reason has once accepted in spite of your changing moods and circumstances."*[32]

And we all know there are many changing moods and circumstances in our workplace.

Key to Senn Delaney's methodology was the inside-out versus outside-in view of change. They grounded us in the reality that preaching or teaching people about the core values would not create culture change. Instead, allowing individuals to experience something, which then enables their convictions to occur, was the route to take.

Through the experiential learning with the culture workshops, people were allowed to see their own behaviors as troublesome and decide to make the change themselves.

Lasting change only happens if the individual decides they want to make the change.

Since culture is inevitably changed one person, one day at a time, and there are a myriad of opportunities to shape it, or it shapes you, then the causal need for individual behavior change is critically important.

However, behavioral change won't last unless thinking becomes a belief, which in turn morphs into faith.

A foundation for all the experiential exercises in Senn Delaney's methodology is called the "Results Cone." It was introduced to us as part of the human operating system, the bedrock for almost everything we worked with people in the workshops to create positive change for business results.

Simply put, to get different results, you need different behaviors. And behaviors will only change when you have a shift in thinking. Creating the opportunity for people to achieve insights through seemingly straightforward exercises enabled them to achieve an "aha" moment that helped begin their inside-out change.

Establishing a core belief system through Our United Culture core values enabled fundamental individual and organizational perspective shifts to undergird the individual's change journey as well. Without the organizational construct of core values for everyone to then marry their personal values to, the notion of organizational "character" doesn't work. For us, the word character meant a lot.

Character gets to the core, whereas personality or spirit comes across as more esoteric.

Going back to our taxonomy, we also discovered ways we could strengthen people as individuals to know themselves better, so they could further develop their own character and more fully contribute to the organization's character.

Personal values and strengths, life purpose statements, and other personal growth development all led to people honestly feeling like the company was investing in them, and the seeds planted in individuals resulted in more organizational alignment.

Culture change is far more than just behavioral modification because you want people to think for themselves rather than comply with a specific targeted behavior. You have to get to the root of their thinking.

Our brains' neural pathways need to be shifted from what currently directs our current behavior to a new pathway that leads to a new behavior.

Our thinking will only consistently shift to the new behavior if we believe the new behavior is worth shifting to because it gets better results.

Internalizing truth enables our actions to flow from our thoughts/beliefs/convictions/faith, even in times of crisis or duress, allowing for much better behavior than we could ever create or with which to comply.

By being intentional and enabling opportunities for people to dig neural pathways through the culture workshops, they could personally appropriate Our United Culture and see a better way of being. Like many things, making the complex simple is a trick, and Senn Delaney helped us get started down that path through the principles they introduced us to in the workshops.

We saw even more effective results when we intentionally declared and linked our truth about the core values to those exercises and stories, so people could more clearly see how their change in behavior would lead to better organizational results.

One truth we learned and leveraged was this reality: Most people don't wake up every day and desire to go into the workplace to mess things up or not work hard.

At least they don't voice those thoughts out loud. They certainly don't type it up and make copies to hand out to others about those negative intentions. Most people want to do a good job and work hard, but our fallible behaviors, along with others' behaviors and situations, combine to create scenarios where people are not at their best. In fact, sometimes they're at their worst.

If you buy into the assumption that people do what makes sense to them, they act upon their beliefs and thoughts, which they feel are rational, logical, and reasonable approaches, then why do things go wrong?

The reality is that fear, control, pride, and selfishness are unfortunately at the core of what triggers most poor behavior.

Therefore, when confronted with others' behaviors not aligned with what makes sense to us, we often respond in hurtful and perhaps even horrible ways. We revert to our own practical or functional core, which is often those negative behaviors. Unless it is clear that those behaviors are not acceptable, and we deliberately work on those behaviors, change will never occur.

Those of you who are parents can probably relate to this well. You don't have to teach a child to be afraid of something. You don't have to teach a child to be selfish. That comes easily to a child. You don't have to teach a child to want to be in control of anything and everything in their surroundings. Focusing on oneself is usually not an issue.

But it takes a lot of time and training to teach children virtuous things. Concepts like respect, dignity, honor, integrity, and trust are areas that take years and years of reinforcement for a child to learn and consistently demonstrate. Ideally, they see these virtues lived out, and they model their behaviors from their parents.

Think about your organization. People from all sorts of backgrounds, all kinds of training, and truckloads of baggage. The best way to give them common ground and like-mindedness is to ground them in what should unify the organization, which are the purpose, mission, and core values of the organization.

Information should be shared, taught, and experienced for people to personally appropriate the desired beliefs and behaviors into their daily activities.

As you approach this lesson, we should all recognize that beliefs are difficult to change, and it won't happen with logic, rationale, or argument. Those usually result only in compliance.

Indeed, some people inevitably will want to alter the belief you have carefully crafted and tried to nurture. We learned that core values can be leveraged, but you will need to stand firm not to alter them.

You can translate them, but don't change them. You can supplement or amplify them, but you don't want to drift from what you've defined as the "truth," the North Star.

Fake news may come in and sound accurate. That's why it's so important to be grounded—so you can spot the fake.

One temptation we faced was trying to stuff too much into the core. We found ourselves trying to shove more in, without our core values context, and thus we constantly battled against dilution. Most of the time, these were worthwhile trainings and teachings, but rather than leveraging the core values into the new trainings and teachings, well-meaning people launched new information without a core values context, which resulted in confusion and frustration.

We'll get to how you'll want to keep your culture fresh in Trail Marker #16, but for now, recognize what you have spent hours working to get personally appropriated, you won't want to pull down by diluting with new information. Keep it simple. You want to build your core values and have enough there for people to readily grab and hold.

Another challenge you'll need to anticipate around the power of belief is that leaders may have spun things so well over the years in negative cultural ways that "the spin" becomes a truth to them and others. Much of this may have evolved from a need to "stay safe" versus being authentically true.

The spin may even have been enhanced by external communications training to protect the organization, and then the messaging gets internally communicated in the same way. The problem is that employees have more access to the broader context of what is happening in the organization and can usually easily see through the spin.

Again, keep it simple.

Questions To Consider

1. What beliefs lie at the root of your organization's core values? How would you articulate those?

2. How much faith exists in your core values to improve your business results? How could you make that more real?

3. How might you introduce new ways of thinking to cause people to shift and change their thinking?

Trail Marker #9

Make It Your Own

"Take ownership. Whatever it takes.
No excuses, no explanations."
Tony Dungy

The organization will need to realize that personal appropriation comes with different ways of viewing the same thing. And that's not only OK, but it should also be encouraged and rewarded. Human beings are not robots. We all have a different set of lenses through which we view the world, and even when we use a common lens of an organizational purpose, mission, and core values, we still have different filters at work, giving us different interpretations. And while some interpretations will need refinement, the overall effect of having each person dig in and appropriate the core values is a huge step forward in advancing your workplace culture.

One theme we stressed during the two-day culture workshop was helping everyone achieve insights in some capacity to shift their thinking and behavior. From there, as mentioned earlier, we ultimately wanted to create faith in the core values. We used stories and exercises to trigger openings to shift their thinking. We also asked a lot of questions. We wanted them to think about how they interpreted and applied the core values. We continually asked:

- How do the core values and principles apply to your work?
- How could you use the core values and principles to get better results?
- How do the core values and principles apply to your personal life?

Kurt Kamph, the Senn Delaney consultant who coached many of us to become certified facilitators, would repeatedly say, "*There's a different way of being that's more fulfilling, and it just works better.*"

The more people thought about and accepted the truth of that statement, the more open they were to shifting their thinking. Personal appropriation of the values is not about creating homogenous, robotic thinking. It's about opening the doors and windows of our minds while being grounded upon a common framework to be like-minded on the essence of how we do what we do, without dictating the application of what we do.

You'll also want to organizationally create unique and distinctive means to enable employees to quickly associate with your core values. Here are three opportunities we saw to do that:

Example #1: When we initially rolled out our core values, we knew we didn't want to just publish them through a memo to all of our people—we wanted to employ the hands-on dynamic we had seen used so successfully in our culture workshops. With Senn Delaney's help, we organized an in-person meeting for the seventy-seven leaders instrumental in helping us identify and define our core values.

We also created, in an incredibly short turnaround timeframe, a brochure capturing all the core values, along with our performance measurement approach, with the names of the seventy-seven leaders in attendance. Our internal Optum Health marketing department created a beautifully effective brochure. Not only was this brochure seen as remarkably creative, but it was also sustained over the next five years, handed out to thousands of our employees, and used by many of us to share with UnitedHealth Group guests. Several of our seventy-seven leaders found it to be so unique that they had the brochure framed for posterity.

Example #2: One benefit we realized with the Senn Delaney approach to culture shaping was their use of posters. Each poster reflected a principle identified in the two-day culture workshops. Many people quickly associated those posters as mechanisms to trigger their thinking back to the workshop experience and the new direction they had adopted. So the posters were powerful tools. For example, the concept of "Be Here Now" on a poster was a direct link to our core value of compassion. By Being Here Now, an individual could demonstrate behaviors reflective of the compassion core value.

But these principles were clearly viewed by our people as originating from Senn Delaney. Even though many were public domain, common usage material, Senn Delaney had done a beautiful job of making them come alive through the culture workshops.

Our CEO quickly recognized our people were associating the Senn Delaney posters in a positive way, but he wanted them to be branded as Our United Culture. Senn Delaney was supportive, so we set out to create Senn Delaney posters, commonly used with all their clients, that were specific and unique to us. Within a matter of weeks, we developed a way to do just that.

As you may recall from Trail Marker #7, we reframed the concepts, tools, and techniques as "principles" to align them within our evolving taxonomy of culture. For each principle, we branded each poster as "Our United Culture. The Way Forward." We then created a "question" to be associated with each principle's visual symbol from the Senn Delaney poster, along with a "hint" to trigger the meaning of each principle.

For example, the question associated with the innovation visual symbol was, "How can I enable more innovation?" The hint was "Stay Curious," which is the essence of the module. We ended up with this format for all twenty-four original Senn Delaney posters, and we also created a few new ones developed by our people over time. You can see these in appendix 2.

Example #3: Shortly after we launched the two-day workshops with our own executives doing the facilitation, one of our culture facilitators approached me with a question of whether I was aware that "homemade" workshops had been created by some of the executives who had gone through the earlier, inaugural workshops.

I wasn't aware, but I was also supportive and thrilled with their actions. When pressed further, I explained, since some executives were compelled to recreate the workshop, based on their workshop experience, their actions simply served to tell me we were definitely on to something.

I followed up with one of the executives spearheading this initiative to see how we might support them in their efforts. He told me he and others recognized it wasn't enough for them as leaders to have personally appropriated the core values; they needed every person in their organization to do the same. To that end, they invested in putting all of their employees through this workshop over several months. He said, "We had to make it our own."

A point bears reinforcing from this story: They were clear that they needed to put *all* their people through the culture workshop. They also then held periodic workshops for new arrivals to ensure everyone had a chance to personally appropriate Our United Culture.

Not everyone in your organization will see it that way, if it's like what we faced at UnitedHealth Group. One of our most senior human capital leaders said, "We've unfrozen enough people; now we can just stop and allow the leaders to work it themselves." Completely wrong approach.

Personal growth never ends, either individually or organizationally. To assume that no more work is needed is akin to assuming that once you've weeded and fertilized the garden, everything will just work out OK for the crops to grow.

Additionally, why would you want to withhold that experience from anyone? Yes, there's a cost, but it's pocket change compared to many other expenditures taking place within your organization. Also, do you want employees who don't fully understand your expectations of them regarding your workplace culture? People are people, and we all make mistakes, forget, get new information, and change our minds. We're constantly changing our perspectives based on new information.

Consider for a moment the people who are not afforded the opportunity to personally embody your core values. They will either drift along with whatever cultural flavor comes to them, *or even worse*, they become dead weight to be carried along by those employees who "get it."

Or even worse, they continue to feed off their misshapen thinking they had before they arrived, and they start to inadvertently influence others away from the like-mindedness you've worked so hard to create.

Or even worse, they intentionally conspire against the organization (some with good intentions) because their thinking is frozen in place and isn't aligned with what the organization espouses.

If you have ever experienced a dysfunctional workplace, it's likely that you haven't had a positive culture experience at a personal level.

Actor Matthew McConaughey, in a commencement address he gave at the University of Houston, sums it up well:

> *"If there's one thing you can depend on people being . . .*
> *it's people. So we shouldn't be surprised.*
> *We . . . us . . . are the trickiest mammals walking on the planet."*[33]

Tricky or not, every person in your organization matters.

And they need to make your culture their own.

Questions To Consider

1. Can you easily tie your cultural values to improving your business? Improving your personal life?
2. What are the sources of the organizational artifacts supporting your culture? Have you made them your own?
3. What are some ways you could start to help everyone in the organization personally experience your culture, if they're not already?

Trail Marker #10

Wins Will Come From Where You Least Expect It

"Sometimes it is the people no one can imagine anything of who do the things no one can imagine."
Alan Turing

The 2014 historical drama *The Imitation Game,* based on the 1983 biography *Alan Turing: The Enigma* by Andrew Hodges, features how an unlikely person, Alan Turing, played a pivotal role in helping the British decrypt German intelligence messages during World War II, thus paving the way for the Allies to achieve key breakthroughs and win the war.

When the challenge of decrypting the German intelligence messages was posed, it was described as Enigma, and in mathematical terms, it was calculated as 159,000,000 × 1,000,000 × 1,000,000 as the daily number of probabilities needed to be ascertained. That translates to twenty years of ten people working 24/7 to figure out the code. A seemingly impossible challenge.

No less so is the challenge in shaping your organizational culture. No matter how many human beings are in your organization, the extrapolated possibilities with the myriad of behaviors and situations each one will encounter daily produce a mathematically mind-numbing, complex problem to solve (remember, they're tricky).

Despite Turing's genius, he encountered failure after failure in deciphering the code. His epiphany comes after overhearing a conversation with a clerical colleague in another department about messages she receives from the same German coder day after day. Turing then realizes he can program the machine he's building to decipher words he already knows exist in certain messages. That "chance" situation led to a breakthrough for Turing and the Allies to successfully break Enigma and proved to be a turning point for World War II.[34]

Similarly, wins and accomplishments in culture transformation often come from where you least expect them.

There's nothing wrong with trying to select great people and employing the 6Ps to get better results. In fact, there is tremendous value in doing that. However, you'll want to keep the door wide open for other possibilities that arise. *People on no one's list and "to-dos" on no one's list could create tremendous applications for your core values.*

Here's a personal example. One weekend I received a call from one of our culture facilitators, Tina. Her voice trembled with emotion as she shared with me what had taken place with her and Anne, her co-facilitator, and one of the participants at their recent workshop in Houston, Texas.

At the start of the workshop, one of the participants, George, was seated at the top left of the horseshoe-shaped assembled chairs, with arms folded and head down, not making eye contact with anyone. Tina approached George as she usually does to welcome participants to the event, and he looked at her and said, "I hope you don't mind, but I really don't want to be here. I have PTSD from the war in Afghanistan, and any time I am in a large group of people, I get nervous and don't feel comfortable talking much." Tina assured him that it was fine, and if at any time he felt uncomfortable, he could simply step out of the room.

The two-day workshop took place without incident, and George left Wednesday afternoon without any comments about whether he had benefited from the workshop or not. He had barely spoken or made any eye contact, and the facilitators couldn't tell whether anything was meaningful for him.

Friday night, Tina and Anne received an email from George with a video presentation, set to music, with coverage on every one of the core values and twenty-four principles they had facilitated in the workshop. It was all stitched together in such a way that it was not only tremendously inspirational but also accurately reflected what had been covered. He had already acquired the music rights, so we could immediately show it to others without infringing on musical copyrights.

Tina said, "Dave, I am stunned! The person I thought would have received the least from the workshop not only absorbed the content, but in about twenty-four hours created this video that brings tears to my eyes. I've never seen anything like it. I just had to call and give you the backstory before I forwarded the video to you."

When I saw it, I was struck with emotion similar to Tina's. The video was so upbeat and positive about the power of what our core values and these principles could accomplish. It is the only time we encountered anything like this out of the roughly thousand workshops we facilitated.

On Monday, I gave George a call to thank him for making and sharing the video with us. I also asked his permission to share it with our culture ambassador community. Unsurprisingly, his answer was, “Of course.” Whatever he could do to help, he felt he was simply there to serve.

Of all the weekly culture digests I sent out to our culture ambassador community, my sharing this story received the most feedback. Many people were moved to tears, and they wanted to get a copy of the video to share with their teams. Of course, George said, “No problem.”

Due to the overwhelming positive response and the exceptional professional quality, we decided to use it as our opening for that year’s annual Culture Ambassador Summit. When people heard the backstory about George and saw the video, they responded with a standing ovation.

The lesson I learned: *Everyone has something to contribute, and what they decide to contribute may not be anything like what is expected or could or should happen.* But if we allow people space and time, they can contribute wonderful things to move others and the organization forward.

Nothing specific was targeted about the timing of this video.

It was simply George’s way of personally appropriating the core values of Our United Culture.

To create a video similar to what George created was on no one’s list.

It was simply the outcome of George’s creatively accountable application.

George himself was not on anyone’s list to target for our culture movement.

He was simply one of the workshop participants invited to join the culture journey.

I had seen the same type of thing occur within Arthur Andersen's demise. During Operation Fight Back, while trying to rally everyone we could to speak up in our defense to politicians and the news media, we weren't getting much information from headquarters in Chicago. The leaders who were supposed to be leading weren't providing much leadership that we could see or feel.

Someone in our Los Angeles office had the idea to picket in front of our building to protest what the Department of Justice was doing to Arthur Andersen. What could be worse than what we were already experiencing? Hmm—not much.

We invited whoever was interested to go down over the lunch hour to wear orange shirts, carry whatever signs they'd like to make, and see if any media might show up to create an angle on the story from our employees' perspective.

Guess who was leading the picketing and the chants? Our janitor, Tony. Someone I never would have imagined getting involved with this was leading the event. In fact, he wasn't even our employee. He was a janitorial service contractor assigned to our floors. His own job wasn't at stake.

After the event ended, I found Tony and asked why he got involved. He responded, "Because I believe what is happening to Andersen is wrong!" Simple and to the point. He believed, and he took action.

Questions To Consider

1. What might be some indicators that you've fallen into the trap of constraining where your business solutions originate?

2. Where might some areas be that you've closed off that you could revisit and perhaps reopen?

Trail Marker #11

Create Communities: Tap Into The Wisdom Of The Teams

"If you want to go fast go alone.
If you want to go far go together."
African Proverb

"Two are better than one, because they have a good return
for their labor: If either of them falls down,
one can help the other up.
A cord of three strands is not quickly broken."
King Solomon

Although many articles and books have been written about the importance and value of creating communities to establish lasting change, we didn't initially think to employ that strategy as part of our culture transformation. Like most lessons we learned, we stumbled into them. However, once we saw how communities could exponentially grow and apply Our United Culture, we tried to leverage it in as many avenues as possible.

While Senn Delaney helped us initiate a culture transformation infrastructure with a culture leadership team (CLT) and culture action team (CAT), we didn't catch on to the power of community to infuse into those teams until we had accidentally discovered the power of the group we called culture ambassadors.

After the fourth culture workshop, three participants, Peter, Andrew, and Mary, asked how they could continue to stay involved in the culture transformation beyond what they had just experienced in the culture workshop. I didn't have any initial ideas, other than to ask them to try to keep their cohort together with encouragement and accountability. As time progressed, and we saw more workshops unfold, other people asked how they could stay involved. I simply put them in touch with Peter, Andrew, and Mary.

About three months later, they came to me again with about thirty people they were supporting with questions, reinforcement, and ideas for applying Our United Culture. By this time, our CLT also saw the need for application and reinforcement through a channel of those individuals who had experienced the culture workshops. Since they were grounded in our core values and principles, we wanted to expand the work of our CATs to see how people might respond to some of those ideas.

I asked Peter, Andrew, and Mary to present to our CLT what they were already doing with this group of people we affectionately named culture ambassadors. By this time, we recognized the importance of nomenclature, so choosing the name was not a quick, default position.

We believed the name "culture ambassador" captured the embodiment of the belief system we tried to implement, and set them apart, so we could easily identify who had volunteered to join.

As culture ambassadors, they have given us permission, by definition, to communicate with them and call upon their help. By placing them in a group outside their regular workday, we empowered them to take action on everything we attempted without needing to seek their supervisor's permission, although we always recommended doing so.

Adam Grant, a Wharton University professor and author, said, "A company isn't a family. Parents don't fire their kids for low performance or furlough them in hard times. A better vision for the workplace is a community—a place where people bond around shared values, feel valued as human beings, and have a voice in decisions that affect them."[35]

Our culture ambassador community grew from the humble beginnings of three people to over twenty-one thousand employees at the time of my departure in January 2019. Established and passionate business leaders led the community, starting with Peter and Mary (Andrew became our lead culture facilitator). We also created a culture ambassador advisory team, which met virtually to discuss the community's needs, and how I and others at the culture office could best support them.

Many elements of the 6Ps were utilized through the culture ambassador community to actively apply Our United Culture.

At one of our monthly culture ambassador broadcasts, we were fortunate to have the Optum chief operating officer join us. During our Q&A time with him, he asked one of our culture ambassador leads, "How many people are you trying to get to become culture ambassadors?"

Without missing a beat, she replied, "Every employee. We would like everyone to be so supportive of Our United Culture that they become a culture ambassador."[36]

While never seen by any of us as a realistic goal, including everyone was our aim. We wanted every employee to feel so connected to our

United Culture that they would not only personally embody the core values, but apply them to everything they did.

We learned that creating a community geared toward action-based shared beliefs and relationships contrasted with the hierarchical corporate structure, which often inadvertently defaulted to action through force, control, and fear.

Aside from our culture ambassador leads and a loose subcommittee of our advisory team, the culture ambassadors had no hierarchy. Everyone was equal. Everyone had the opportunity to share what they were doing to actively apply and reinforce Our United Culture.

Nothing was imposed on them. Rather, ideas were suggested and testimonials were given to help them see the possibilities that could exist with Our United Culture. People who had never met one another instantly bonded when they identified as culture ambassadors. Ideas and opinions were exchanged freely, and the community grew.

We also learned that people wanted to join the culture ambassador community, but the initial threshold to join was to go through the two-day culture workshop. Earlier, we decided that one qualification needed to become a culture ambassador was to become grounded in the core values and principles to gain a common language and understanding.

We were constrained on the supply side (workshops), which also caused a default on the demand side, as those not senior enough were unable to gain entrance to the workshops. Since we were already learning wins were coming from unexpected places, we decided to begin allowing anyone to join who would become grounded by going through two ninety-minute webinars.

We immediately saw a significant increase in our culture ambassador community growth, along with more ideas and possibilities for active application. The community developed a reputation for being people who would listen, learn, and apply whatever was introduced to them.

Doers, not cheerleaders.

As long as we began with the foundation of our core values, we realized we could activate this community toward any business initiative our business leaders designated.

Another community core to our sustainability was the culture facilitator community. Culture facilitators were senior executives who volunteered to undergo extensive grounding to lead the two-day culture workshops and the one-day follow-up reinforcement workshops. This was a significant time investment for the individuals, along with a financial investment by our organization.

Initially, sixteen of us volunteered and were taken through the process by Senn Delaney. We learned a lot about organizational culture, and most importantly, we learned more about ourselves and how we might influence the organizational culture. We realized we had to individually change even more to guide other people to arrive at their insights.

We ended up with over 250 facilitators we put through this process. Many of the culture facilitators said things like, "Becoming a culture facilitator was one of the hardest and best things I've ever done in the world. It's the reason I stayed at UnitedHealth Group."

Relationships were built, and those relationships led to genuine friendships and impacted business results. While being a culture facilitator was a lot of work and definitely did feel good, we believed the business case for relationships being strengthened would help the organization's overall health.

We learned that when you're in a community, you gain tremendous commitments. Everything, from as seemingly small as getting an accountability/encouragement partner to the broader range of recognition within those communities, plays a part.

Given the significant time and financial investment being made in our culture facilitators, we recognized their accomplishment each year with a graduation dinner. Senior leaders from the businesses were also invited to attend. One of our most senior culture facilitators was a long-time Executive Vice President for UnitedHealth Group, Janet.

Janet had served in many CEO and functional roles within our organization and was commonly recognized as doing Our United Culture before Our United Culture existed. She graciously offered to host the dinner at her home each year. What started out as a graduation recognition dinner grew to become an opportunity to nurture and engage the culture facilitator community.

For recognition, we gave each newly-certified culture facilitator a letter signed by our CEO. For the initial sixteen facilitators, he also handwrote a brief comment below the letter.

For me, he wrote, "We would never be where we are in this today—without your dedication and leadership—not even close. It's like you were born for this—I can't thank you enough. But keep it going."[37]

To say I was inspired and motivated by this would be a vast understatement.

Three other communities emerged as our culture ambassador community grew. Two culture ambassadors from the innovation department wanted to attract like-minded people who were voracious about our innovation core value. They created a group called "innovation advocates" with two requirements:

- A person had to be grounded with Our United Culture

- They had to go through additional grounding on innovation techniques.

Both were easy and quick to accomplish.

From there, as we saw a need to focus on diversity and inclusion, so we created a subgroup of culture ambassadors, similar to innovation advocates, and we called them "relationship builders." We developed foundational grounding on our relationship's core value and quickly attracted people interested in knowing and pursuing more. Since volunteers did not organically start this group, we asked three senior culture facilitators if they could volunteer to lead the group. All said yes!

As both groups grew, a third community got started. Two human resource professionals wanted to improve the foundational knowledge of sound change management across the enterprise. Thus, "change makers" were born. They quickly grew to over five hundred members.

Essential to all of the communities, we created two attributes:

- *Inclusive*: Every community was open to anyone who wanted to join.
- *Voluntary*: No one was assumed, required, or pressured to join.

The only common requirement? Become grounded in Our United Culture as a culture ambassador.

Over the nine years I served in the culture office, we formed multiple communities from 2010 to 2018, all of which played significant roles in accountably applying Our United Culture:

- Culture leadership teams, at the UHG, UHC, and Optum levels
- Culture action teams
- Culture ambassadors

- Culture ambassador advisory team
- Culture facilitators
- Culture facilitator coaches
- Innovation advocates
- Relationship builders
- Change makers

To tap into the wisdom of the teams, you've got to have teams.

Create 'em and turn 'em loose.

Questions To Consider

1. What teams in your organization already exist? Could you empower them even more?
2. Could "extracurricular" teams be created specifically to advance your organization's culture?

Trail Marker #12

Trust The Process

"Not all who wander are lost."
J.R.R. Tolkien

"Great things are done by a series of small things brought together."
Vincent Van Gogh

The culture journey outcome probably won't be what you think, but with proper grounding for your people, it will exceed your expectations. I was continually amazed at how extraordinary lasting results can begin with simple steps.

The phrase "trust the process" became meaningful to me when I went through the six-month process to become a culture facilitator. The endgame was daunting. Fifteen of my colleagues and I were given two thick binders containing the content covered in the two-day culture workshops, and we needed to become familiar enough with it to expertly facilitate a group of thirty people over two days.

Factually, we knew the Senn Delaney culture facilitators each benefited from years of experience with the materials. But especially challenging to each of us was the intangible outcome. They had demonstrably struck chords in our hearts and minds, inspiring us to be part of the transformation effort as culture facilitators, and we all wondered how we could pull that off.

We were constantly told through the six-month timeframe to "trust the process." And of course, whenever our instructors used that phrase, it was done with an insightful, knowing "look" that didn't leave us feeling comfortable. Additionally, we were told not to memorize the binder materials. We were to become "grounded" in the material and "trust the process."

"Trust the process" is a fundamental phrase for the organizational culture-shaping process. A good illustration for this phrase comes from the 1984 hit movie, *The Karate Kid*.[38] Near the beginning of the film, Daniel, the new kid at school, is getting beaten up by a group of bullies when an elderly Japanese man, Mr. Miyagi, seemingly comes out of nowhere using karate strikes to thrash the bullies and send them packing.

Daniel is duly impressed and asks Mr. Miyagi to teach him karate so he can defend himself. Mr. Miyagi agrees to do so if Daniel will simply follow his instructions and not question them. Daniel agrees, and Mr. Miyagi, over the course of four days, gives him four grueling household chores:

- Wax the cars—wax on with a right-hand circular motion, wax off with a left-hand circular motion
- Sand the decks—right circle, left circle, all while pressing down to sand the deck

- Paint the fence—long stroke up, long stroke down. Focus on the wrist
- Paint the house—long stroke right side, long stroke left side. Focus on the wrist.

By the end of the fourth day, Daniel is extremely frustrated as he doesn't see how doing these menial jobs filled with repetitive tasks is going to help him learn karate.

Mr. Miyagi responds by telling Daniel to defend himself. Miyagi then proceeds to attack Daniel with strikes and kicks. Daniel's defensive muscle memory springs into action using the movements ingrained through the household chores he performed. Daniel learned to trust the process Mr. Miyagi used to teach karate.

Similarly, the grounding approach for culture facilitators, the two-day culture workshop exercises and reflections, and the ongoing daily individual character demonstration throughout the organization are all examples of trusting the process.

Here are a few of the truisms the phrase represents:

- You don't know what will trigger an insight for every person, and that's OK.
- You don't know what will stick with a person post-workshop, and that's OK.
- Each person will process what is introduced differently, and that's OK.
- The material is structured to allow a person to face their thought habits in a non-judgmental way.

- Most of the workshop will be fluid based on how the participants respond, but you must be specific with instructions in a few spots.

Not only did I find "trust the process" to work in grounding us as culture facilitators, I also found it to be true in applying Our United Culture. Here's one example.

We were four years along in our journey to transform our corporate culture based on our five core values of integrity, compassion, relationships, innovation, and performance.

I had heard about a business initiative in our Medicare and Retirement (M&R) division to frame the month of February around our compassion core value, which we defined as "walking in the shoes of the people we serve and those with whom we work."

The primary focus of the initiative involved the three thousand consumer advocates who daily served our members on the phone, responding to their questions and concerns. These consumer advocates were each being asked to handwrite five thank-you notes to members they spoke to in February.

This was a considerable task, because when M&R members call us, they're not calling because they're pleased with something. They're usually anxious, angry, fearful, or confused.

Additionally, with our call centers focused on metrics around average handle time, average speed to answer, and first-call resolution, to have our consumer advocates take time away from the phones to write thank-you notes was a risk to our standard key performance indicators.

I had heard good things about the initiative, so in the role I served in supporting the progress of Our United Culture, I asked Valerie, the operations leader responsible for the initiative, to lunch to hear more about it.

Valerie shared with me some hoops she had to jump through to clear the new process with HR, legal, and marketing. She also shared that the only things given to the consumer advocates were a pen, paper, envelopes, and stamps. Many requested a script, but they were told to simply express the compassion value in their own words to the members in a grateful manner.

Valerie then leaned forward and said, "Dave, you want to know the most amazing thing about the whole process?"

"Of course," I said.

She was almost giddy. "Dave, the members have started writing back!"

"In fact, here's one of the thank-you notes Joe received from one of our members. It read,

'Dear Joe,

Thank you for sending that wonderful note. I never received anything like that from a business of any kind. You went the extra mile, and it really meant a lot to me and my family. Again, thank you for really caring.

Love, Marge.'"

She continued, "Dave, we're getting notes like this back every day. Also, some of the members are even sending gifts and fruit baskets to our consumer advocate call centers.

"This process has worked so well that we've incorporated thank-you notes as part of our customer experience process. To date, we've sent over sixty thousand handwritten thank-you notes, and other divisions are now utilizing the same process with their members and customers."

Valerie sparked her culture in an amazing way with this active application. She ignited and fueled lasting results—one person, one day, one step at a time.

A couple of years later, we received what we felt was an incredible testament to trusting the process with the fortitude and stickiness of Our United Culture. Sheryl Skolnick, an analyst with Mizuho Financial, publicly made this observation about UHG following the 2016 Investor Day:

It is a remarkable thing, this transformation of UnitedHealth.

It's been a transformation not only of business model, but of culture and mission. We've watched, over the twenty or so years that we've covered the company for one firm or another, the story and the people change and grow.

And like our families, UNH has matured and seasoned. It's gone through brash teen years, a rebellious college period when wild options were sown, and then through a period of epiphany and rebirth during which it remade itself—culturally, operationally, and strategically.

In our view, UNH has transformed again, has come of age, and looks to be fulfilling the promise we first saw seven years ago.[39]

Note: Our first culture workshop was held in December 2009.

Questions To Consider

1. Where might you need to stretch to "trust the process" for organizational results?
2. What examples could you share where a leader has applied your organizational core values to a business process?

Trail Marker #13

Say Yes To Everything: Don't Let The "No's" Have It!

"If somebody offers you an amazing opportunity, but you are not sure you can do it, say yes— then learn how to do it later.

Richard Branson

Richard Sheridan, CEO of Menlo Innovations, a small software company in Ann Arbor, Michigan, is the author of the book *Joy, Inc.* In it, he describes how Menlo shaped their culture and how any organization can form passionate teams and achieve lasting results. He says, "Part of the vulnerability of not having all the answers is the humility to share your ideas with your team before they're fully formulated."

Unlike many leaders who feel they need to have all the answers for all the problems they face, Richard encourages and expects team members to solve the problems. He states, "Freedom from fear requires feeling safe. If you feel safe, you run experiments. You stop asking permission.

You avoid long, mind-numbing meetings. You create a new kind of culture in which you accept the mistakes are inevitable. You learn that small, fast mistakes are preferable to the big, slow, deadly mistakes you're making today."[40]

This approach is a significant shift from what happens at many organizations, where the essence is, "We'll tell you when we need you, so just keep your head down and keep working until we call you." For years, UnitedHealth Group had been this kind of company. Our United Culture, which includes the innovation core value, marked a significant change to that approach. But old habits die hard.

Giving up control is difficult for most leaders because they think they need to be pushing the button or making a decision. The reality is you may have an illusion of control, but beneath the 6Ps are fully functioning people making a myriad of daily decisions you'll never even know exist, let alone control. For example, many times, people turnover catches leaders by surprise, because they think they're in control and everything is going well, when the reality is their employees are disengaged and unfulfilled.

For several years, I've received chiropractic treatment from Dr. Mike. I've learned that an analogy of cause and effect is easier to see with his adjustments of my joints, but also giving me exercises to shape my muscles to help keep the bones in place. He likens it to strings controlling a puppet. There's always a cause or correlation, but many times it's difficult to see.

For him to best adjust my neck, I need to trust him enough to let my head rest freely in his hands and give him complete control. My natural tendency, however, is to protect or compensate where my neck may be having the most trouble. Short-term, before the adjustment, I feel constrained and uncomfortable, but long-term, this adjustment is necessary to heal and fully function.

Another way to think about this approach is by reviewing a golfer's swing. As a below-average player, I learned that the golf grip needs to be gentle but firm. For a right-handed player, the left hand is the only one needed to achieve power in the swing. The right hand is there to merely guide the swing and should be held loosely around the left hand and club, utilizing enough influence to provide accuracy to the shot.

An early recollection I have of this insight came from our Texas business in the Medicaid space. Their leader, Nancy, reached out to me after having gone through a culture workshop and immediately wanted to have her entire four-hundred-person organization experience the workshop. I could not say yes to her initial request due to resource constraints. She then asked if she could create a workshop based on what she had learned from her experience. I said yes and gave her access to the content we had, thinking they might cobble together a two- to three-hour workshop.

You can imagine my surprise when, a month later, Nancy invited me to their inaugural two-day workshop. I was blown away by the amazing work they had done. One of our Culture Facilitators, Marie, recalled I had told them, "There is no wrong or right way to do workshops with your people. You just have to do what's real and genuine for you. Your audience will let you know."

And wow, at the kickoff, did their audience ever let them know. What a resounding success! The authenticity, transparency, and vulnerability the leaders exhibited while sharing their groundings were exceptional.

What would've happened if I had said no to them creating their workshop? What if I just told them to wait until we could get to them, and I could get more resources?

First, the solution would never have been as quick.

Second, having the audience know the senior leaders leading the workshop generated an authenticity second to none.

And third, the relationships coalescing around the common goal of the business improvements needed were incredible.

Months later, I circled back to Nancy to see how the business and workshops were going and how Our United Culture may have contributed to their results. Nancy stated that Our United Culture was the impetus for all the business strategies and tactics they successfully utilized to improve our business in the state of Texas. It's a good thing we didn't say no.

Saying yes to everything doesn't mean you say yes to things you think would do harm to the business; however, many leaders take too hard a line in what they think harm is.

They end up battling against the "not invented here" syndrome. If you can't be open to the fact that you don't have all the answers, then you won't be successful in getting the transformation you'd like to see.

Another battle to be had is going for progress, not perfection. If you wait till you think you'll get it "just right," that moment will never come. Accept anyone willing to contribute toward the goal and give them some resources and tools along the way, and you'll be pleasantly surprised with the outcome.

Another example of us saying yes to everything was the approval process for senior leaders to become culture facilitators. Our culture office accepted everyone we were given if the base criteria of interest and availability were met. No fancy talent management grid gave us the "right" people. We wanted people who wanted to be part of the change.

We wanted people who felt compelled to do this work—they simply could not "not do" this. We found referrals from other culture facilitators to be the best forecaster of future success for our candidates in executing the workshops, living out the core values, and actively applying Our United Culture. We learned to trust the culture facilitator community to know who would work best.

Questions To Consider

1. Have you ever been told no on an idea you had without being given sound logic for that answer? If so, how did that make you feel?
2. What are some things you might have said no to that perhaps you could reconsider?
3. What are some new ideas you could immediately say yes to and see what happens?

Trail Marker #14

Culture Dissonance

"Dissonance cannot be corrected by criticism.
Dissonance . . . is like darkness in a room.
It does little good to scold the darkness.
We must displace the darkness by introducing light."
WILFORD W. ANDERSON

Every year, UnitedHealth Group hosts an annual leadership gathering comprising approximately one thousand of our most senior executives. Over the years, this event has evolved from a half-day with the CEO sharing the state of the business and other divisional CEOs bombarding us with PowerPoints to a couple of days filled with team problem-solving, inspirational speakers, leadership development, and time with a service project for nonprofit organizations.

After Our United Culture came into existence, our CEO was open to utilizing the values and tactical principles at the Leadership Gathering to support the senior leaders working together on problem-solving common business issues facing the various UHG platforms.

Our 2014 Leadership Gathering was shaping up like many others, with breakout sessions utilizing our values and principles, along with other team dynamic models, to help advance our thinking on some common issues. We had approximately ten executives on every team, addressing eight overall business problems with about twelve teams on each problem.

Before we began the breakout working sessions, the business issue sponsor gave an overview of the issue being addressed to add color commentary to the facts and data given to each team. After hearing from the last sponsor on the last business issue, our CEO, Robert took the stage.

We all assumed Robert would simply wrap up the overviews with encouragement and admonition to work hard and follow the process, so we could get better results. We were all shocked, however, when he took the ninth business issue about cultural dissonance and told all the teams to work on this problem as well as their other assigned problem. He wanted results submitted on each business issue, including the cultural dissonance issue.

Basically, he told us he had articulated what he wanted Our United Culture to be. However, he had been hearing we were not living out what we said we wanted to be. He wanted to know why and how we would change. He didn't care about fingers being pointed; he wanted solutions to be proposed, so we could aggressively pursue the way forward.

For those of us on the culture leadership team (CLT) and our facilitator community, we could hardly believe our ears. Robert had just teed up Our United Culture front and center far more than we had seen in the last couple of years. While many of us saw and heard about this culture dissonance, it was an elephant-in-the-room issue.

Robert further stated that when the results of the culture dissonance solutions were received, the executive team would review all the results and declare a winner. The winning team would then take all of the solutions offered and create an overall culture-shaping plan to address the culture dissonance challenge.

Many ideas were offered through a long list of proposed solutions, ranging from short-term tactics to long-range strategies. The winning team happened to have one of our CLT members and a culture facilitator as the co-lead. They enthusiastically embraced the process and developed an overall plan, all of which the executive team supported.

The plan emphasized leadership as a privilege to serve, not a right to be in charge. You can see the plan's overarching themes and summary and recommendations in appendix 3.

The culture dissonance problem-solving benefited far more than just those ten recommendations. The full inventory of ideas and suggestions was given to the culture office, along with our culture ambassador leads, to see how we could weave them into whatever processes we could along the way. The groundswell of recognition and support for Our United Culture was extraordinary.

No matter the size of your organization, as we've previously discussed, human beings are the trickiest mammals on the planet. *Regardless of good intentions, solid execution, and even appealing notoriety, inevitable dissonance will occur*. The nobility of living out corporate values is simply beyond any organization's continual capacity and should be revisited.

Constantly revisiting the expectations around the core values and publicly pulling the most senior leaders into the solutioning process gave a wonderful lift to Our United Culture along our journey. The additional focus did not cost a significant amount of out-of-pocket dollars, just the opportunity cost of our executives' time on a topic that further leveraged their abilities to solve more problems in the way we wanted.

The following year at our 2015 Leadership Gathering, Robert reminded everyone of the 2014 Culture Dissonance challenge and shared the themes and recommendations being implemented from the work of 2014's winning team. He encouraged us to take personal accountability for Our United Culture and recognize the emphasis on culture was not going away but was deepening in our resolve to better live out our mission and core values.

Questions To Consider

1. What is the current state of your organization's culture? Is there a noticeable dissonance, and if so, what are you willing to do about it?

2. Could any of the potential solutions listed in appendix 3 potentially be useful?

3. Are you willing to allow the business culture to be addressed by the business leaders, and not just departments? The departments should be supporting the process, but not driving it. Business leaders need to own their culture.

Trail Marker #15

Spring Training

"People who write about spring training not being necessary have never tried to throw a baseball."

Sandy Koufax

If you're a baseball fan, odds are high the mention of spring training immediately brings all sorts of positive thoughts flooding into your mind. Perhaps it signals the end of a dreary winter, the expectant anticipation of your favorite player working out the kinks, the inspiring story of a minor leaguer doing what it takes to make the big leagues, or the advent of another season full of drama and excitement with your home team.

However, most of what is chronicled for a current Major League Baseball (MLB) player's point of view involves their thoughts as an unpaid requirement to get back into shape and prove their worth to make the current season's roster.

They don't get to do anything new. They simply do what they've done since they were kids playing baseball in the backyard: throw, hit, field, and run as they play through multiple games and situational scenarios throughout the day.

History tells us spring training started in 1870 with the Cincinnati Red Stockings and the Chicago White Stockings holding organized baseball camps in New Orleans, making it almost as old as baseball itself. And from the beginning, all players were required to participate.

From the start of our culture journey, Senn Delaney made it clear to sustain the core values and principles, you had to solve real business problems using them. Simply adding them on as decorations at the end of business solutioning was not the answer.

However, like many organizations and people, to continually revisit and put practice around situations was almost unheard of and certainly not practical. Even though we continually like to refer to sporting analogies of how practice makes perfect and perfect practice makes perfect, the reality of practicing anything we put into play was virtually nonexistent. The only exception I've ever heard is sales teams practicing and rehearsing sales delivery pitches.

Keith, one of our culture facilitators and a senior executive in the Medicare space, consistently used the analogy of spring training to get the point across. When players go to spring training for baseball, what do they do? They don't invent new things for the sport. They practice hitting, fielding, and throwing. Then they practice scenarios from real games to help them think through how they're going to respond to those situations.

For Our United Culture, we needed to do the same thing. We needed to use the fundamentals of our culture and apply them against real-world business problems we were facing, so we actually have the opportunity to see Our United Culture at work and advance the journey. Our CEO, Robert, listened to Keith and took action.

As our featured guest for our December 2015 culture ambassador call, Robert announced,

> *"I am looking to do—my term for this will be a "surge," to now make another thrust into culture. I'd like to do that in 2016 and formulate a plan of action about bringing another bolt of energy to this, and to also make sure this is done at the very roots of the organization. So that everybody who comes into the organization gets really grounded in this, so that it's said twenty years from now—this is just how we think and operate here."*[41]

After quickly consulting with Robert about exactly what he was looking for, he sent out a memo to the executive leadership team and instructed them that sometime in the next six months, they needed to organize and put into play a "principles workout" that one of our culture facilitators would facilitate. These workouts needed to be focused on real-world problems and involve the appropriate members of the natural work teams necessary to solve those problems.

Our culture office, along with a few of our most senior culture facilitators, put together what this day could look like. While revisiting the principles in rapid-fire fashion, the bulk of the day was spent utilizing the values and principles in a problem-solving way. As Keith liked to say,

"You're going to show up to do some work in the best way possible. We're simply ensuring some of our culture principle tools are embedded to help you do it most effectively and efficiently. We're here to do real work, not fluffy add-ons."[42]

While we didn't know the cognitive psychosis at the time, we implemented B.F. Skinner's teachings: "The strengthening of behavior which results from reinforcement is appropriately called 'conditioning.'

In operant conditioning, we strengthen an operant in the sense of making a response more probable or, in actual fact, more frequent."[43]

We then beta-tested this approach with Robert's select group of leaders as part of a leadership development group.

The results were outstanding. Not only did our CEO, the senior team, and this leadership group wholeheartedly endorse the process, but the first several real-world issues we worked on made amazing strides in advancing toward viable solutions.

I'd like to tell you there was an amazing secret sauce to its success, but it wasn't anything more than applying the fundamentals and taking the time to work through them. Even some of our most grounded culture facilitators were amazed at the success they had with their natural work teams in applying these with an outside culture facilitator.

One team I facilitated included our UHG COO, our CIO, and several of the divisional CFOs. All of them concluded we made more progress in six hours than had been made in the previous six weeks. They were amazed.

The principles workouts became the new way of advancing the ball on major issues UnitedHealth Group faced. While not applied consistently, enough leaders incorporated the fundamentals to continue the journey of Our United Culture in a fresh way.

Questions To Consider

1. What are some of the biggest problems facing your business that could use a fresh approach, reminiscent of spring training?

2. Do your values and culture approach provide the requisite fundamentals to enable spring training? If not, how might you strengthen or expand your approach to do "real work" with your culture?

Trail Marker #16

Three Mainstays: Real, Relevant, Real-Time

"Only a man's character is the real criteria of worth."
ELEANOR ROOSEVELT

What is the most popular sport in the world? If your answer was futbol (aka soccer), you are correct. And not by a small margin either. The sport has roughly 3.5 billion fans worldwide and 250 million players across two hundred countries around the world. The next most popular sport in the world is cricket, with 2.5 billion fans, basketball with 2.2 billion fans, and field hockey with a mere two billion fans.[44]

Growing up in Kansas in the 1960s, I did not become familiar with the game of soccer until I reached college. Up to that point, soccer seemed like a boring sport. After all, the whole game is merely kicking a ball up and down the field while trying to kick it into a goal. Dull, plain, and unimaginative.

However, when I was asked to coach my kids' teams in the late '90s, and I started reading books about how to be an effective youth soccer coach, I learned just how exciting, sophisticated, and incredibly imaginative the game could be.

Or, as Dani Rojas from the hit show *Ted Lasso* proclaims, "Futbol is life!"[45]

So how, as a youth coach, could I help kids gain the "futbol is life" view and not see the game as dull and plain? On one level, I didn't have to do anything but throw the ball onto the field and ask the kids to kick it. There's something amazingly attractive about a bouncing ball to most young kids.

On the other hand, the more the kids grew in their skills around the fundamentals of foot skills, dribbling, and kicking placement, the more creative they became in how they played the game. Additionally, when new skills and ideas were introduced, I saw different kids latch on to different ideas to help them grow in their skills and abilities. Different strokes for different folks.

I'm sure the same could be said about many sports. While fundamentals remain the same, the growth and skills are negated only by the lack of imagination and creativity by coaches and players.

The same could be said for organizational culture. The fundamentals we've discussed in the previous chapters need to remain sound. But they don't have to be boring; they should get lots of repetition, and they should never be redundant.

Keeping your culture fresh should be a primary focus for your culture to thrive.

As mentioned, our culture journey at UnitedHealth Group began with Senn Delaney, the corporate culture consulting firm. They got us started by utilizing their standard approach in culture shaping.

Our CEO was adamant and relentless in telling me and others to ensure Our United Culture didn't just become a Senn Delaney cookie-cutter culture. Of course, the core values and definitions we chose were unique. But the principles used to reinforce those core values were the Senn Delaney model.

So under his mandate, and our CLT's guidance, we immediately began looking for ways to keep Our United Culture fresh, thus evolving into an organism only found at UnitedHealth Group. So while the fundamentals around our values, and the principles around living those values, remained in place throughout our journey, we continuously built upon them by introducing new perspectives, in addition to actively showing new applications of them as well.

In addition to the soccer analogy used earlier, also try thinking of vitamin supplements to strengthen your organizational culture. You need to eat balanced meals to keep your foundation solid, but different situations and people need different experiences to supplement their diet.

Or if you use a cooking analogy, your main ingredient in cooking a dish may remain the same, but with the hundreds of different spices available, you can flavor it uniquely and deliciously for different palates.

Additionally, with corporate culture, you need to feed what you've planted. No matter how successful you were with your initial grounding of the values you've committed to, if your corporate culture is merely seen as a required workshop, or worse yet, a training, the shelf life won't be long. As pointed out, applying and regularly reinforcing your values in real business scenarios is the best way to advance your culture.

As a rallying message to help us keep it fresh, our UnitedHealthcare CEO encouraged us to keep it real, relevant, and real-time. We built upon this phrase for Our United Culture to be:

- Real—Nothing fake, fully authentic
- Relevant—Directly useful to getting better results
- Real-time—Immediately applicable, not to sit in a toolbox for a rainy day

We didn't immediately realize what all of that could look like, but under that banner, we began to see how to contribute tangibly to the ongoing growth of Our United Culture. Here are a few additional mechanisms or approaches we incorporated to further cultivate Our United Culture.

First, I'll cover some of the different thought leaders we brought into Our United Culture to share their perspectives, which deepened either our understanding and application of one of the core values or broadened our views around how the values and principles could be applied. Then I'll share some of the avenues we used to further cultivate our culture.

Early on, we recognized that for people to strongly align with our organizational core values, they needed to understand clearly their personal core values. To that end, we brought in my good friend John Blumberg, an author, speaker, and former colleague of mine from Arthur Andersen. John was the keynote speaker at our first culture ambassador summit and utilized an exercise to help people determine their personal core values and then link those to the organizational values of Our United Culture.

At my oldest son's university commencement, I heard David Horsager speak. David is the author of a book called *The Trust Edge*. While I was looking forward to getting a quick nap during the commencement address, I found myself furiously taking notes on what David was saying.

We ended up bringing David in as a keynote speaker and consultant as we worked to deepen our relationship core value, which we had defined as "build trust through collaboration."

Much like Senn Delaney had introduced us to a tangible way to approach an ambiguous topic like culture, David had developed eight pillars to tangibly build trust with others. He became a wonderful partner and friend.

Later in our journey, we were introduced to Richard Leider, commonly known as the godfather of personal purpose. Richard has written over twelve books and invested over forty years in dealing with the topic of personal purpose. We were looking for ways for individuals to more clearly understand their purpose and align it to our overall organizational mission, much like we had done with the core values. Richard became a trusted seer into our approach and was remarkably adaptive in the way he used his research and writings to advance Our United Culture.

We also tapped into Gallup, Inc. with StrengthsFinder. Similar to John's and Richard's work, we wanted people to use their individual strengths and knowledge to better advance Our United Culture. Becoming more familiar with their personal strengths enabled better communication between individuals and helped people see more clearly how they could advance their competencies.

Shawn Achor, a former Harvard University professor and author of the books *Happiness Advantage* and *Big Potential*, also contributed to keeping Our United Culture fresh. He delivered keynotes at several of our Culture Ambassador Summits and also assisted with a few of our monthly culture ambassador calls. His research and findings on how the pursuit and joy of fulfilling your potential helped many of our people engage more actively with Our United Culture.

Paul Batz, originator of the Good Leadership breakfast, author, and leadership coach, also helped us utilize his tools and techniques to further supplement Our United Culture. His work around the seven Fs (faith, family, finances, fitness, friends, fun, future) greatly helped people see work as not just a balance, but a blend—a blend to be managed to have an effective and fulfilling purpose.

All these people and their organizations helped us further refine, evolve, and shape Our United Culture in real, relevant, and real-time ways. I'm sure there are others who could be useful to you and your organization—the key to remember is they need to supplement your core and not be confused by the organization as a different "flavor of the month."

Here is an extension to the agricultural and cooking analogies: Too much of any good thing can cause results to dissipate. For example, too much salt in a recipe could destroy it or potentially distract from the main ingredients. Similarly, too much fertilizer could have a negative impact on your crops.

You'll want to supplement your values, not supplant them.

Use your values to label these new items, link them back to your values, and then leverage your new ingredients deeper into the organization.

Whether farming, cooking, or culture, there's a need to feed.

Questions To Consider

1. What are your initial thoughts on how you might supplement your existing culture?
2. Do you agree or disagree with the statement, "Repetition isn't redundancy"? Why or why not?

Trail Marker #17

The Paradox Of Cultural Leadership

"Who you are speaks so loudly I can't hear what you're saying."
Ralph Waldo Emerson

I came across a few factoids about the number of leadership books in print today. At the time, one source cited four leadership books per day being published. Another source shared that Amazon offers 57,136 books with the word "Leadership" in the title. Whatever the actual numbers are, many leadership books are available with many different opinions, tools, strategies, behavioral concepts, pillars, two-by-two grids, styles, types, theories, essentials, surveys, stories, statistics, documented studies, and *more.*

Why so many, and which ones are the "best"? I don't want to wade into speculation. I've read many useful books about leadership, and many nuggets helped me navigate the different organizations, situations, and people I've had the opportunity to work with over my career. I'm sure you have as well. And whatever truisms, characteristics, lessons, and principles you've found useful, you'll need them all in working to shape your organizational culture.

I will not try to espouse or replicate any specific leadership book, but this book wouldn't be complete without sharing our learnings about leadership attributes we encountered while working to shape our corporate culture.

Based on what you've read so far, you may be thinking, "Well, since it seems that everything everywhere in an organization can affect its culture, then all activities of a leader will lend themselves toward shaping its culture." You are correct.

If you want to fully transform your culture by developing its character and reaping better results, we noticed some specific leadership attributes that seemed to be more effective than others. These attributes showed up in a wide variety of people living out their beliefs in a wide variety of scenarios and situations.

The common thread I'd draw your attention to: leadership never points back to itself, but always to advance Our United Culture—what we termed as the organizational culture embodied by our character and defined by our core values.

First, you guessed it; let's define what we're actually talking about when we talk about leadership. Similar to Trail Marker #2 with definitions of corporate culture, many useful definitions exist. Here are a few about leaders and leadership that stand out to me, particularly with a bent toward leading culture transformation:

- Tom Wilson, Allstate CEO: "Leadership is getting people to willingly go someplace they wouldn't go themselves."[46]

- Gen. H. Norman Schwarzkopf: "Leadership is a combination of strategy and character. If you must be without one, be without the strategy."[47]
- John Maxwell: "Your walk talks louder than your talk talks."[48]
- Admiral Grace Murray Hooper, US Navy: "You manage things, you lead people."[49]
- Lao Tse, Tao Te Ching: "The superior leader gets things done with very little motion. He imparts instruction not through many words but through a few deeds. He keeps informed about everything but interferes hardly at all. He is a catalyst, and though things would not get done well if he weren't there, when they succeed, he takes no credit. And because he takes no credit, credit never leaves him."[50]
- Warren Bennis: "A leader doesn't just get the message, he is the message."[51]
- Peter Drucker: "Management is doing things right; leadership is doing the right things."[52]
- Afghan proverb: "If you think you are leading, and no one is following you, then you are only taking a walk."[53]

Additionally, the foundational cultural leadership principle we gleaned from Senn Delaney was that "over time, organizations tend to take on the characteristics of their leaders."[54]

Well-known examples include Jack Welch with GE, Walt Disney with Disney, Herb Kelleher with Southwest Airlines, Sam Walton with Walmart, and Elon Musk with Tesla. Larry Senn coined this principle with the "Leadership Shadow." Expressed in behavioral terms, it's "What you permit is what you promote."[55]

I recently came across a leadership descriptor that also fits what I had observed at UnitedHealth Group in our culture-shaping efforts. It's called Congruent Leadership, shared by Jon Michael, CEO of The Image Group, "Where the activities, actions, and deeds of the leader are matched by and driven by their values and beliefs about [in this case] care and nursing."[56] Overall, it's where leaders find their mark on beliefs, principles, and values.

Inc. magazine points out, "Congruence is what separates the most influential leaders from everyone else. And here's why, without it, you're just like everyone else."[57]

To frame a few upcoming cultural leadership perspectives,
here's my definition of cultural leaders:
A cultural leader selflessly lives out beliefs and values
to influence others toward the organizational common cause.

Let's specifically define what this statement means, with what comes to mind with the words describing this leader:

Selfless. Puts the needs of others ahead of self. Stays grounded on the core. Clear where they stand and where they're going.

- No self-promotion or prestige.
- Values relationships for what they are, not for what they give.
- What you see is what you get, and you like and respect what you see and get.
- Aware that blind spots exist and readily accepts counsel.

Lives out beliefs and values. Courage of convictions. Challenges the status quo logically and practically.

- Practice what they preach.
- Walk talks louder than talk talks.
- Avoids hypocrisy.
- Congruence of beliefs/values and behaviors/actions.
- Never phased by sudden or abrupt changes. They know established core values and cultural principles will guide them through.
- Acknowledges shortfalls and works to improve.

Influence others. People are drawn to their authenticity, transparency, and action.

- Diplomatic but not a politician. They do whatever it takes to do the right thing, not just to get ahead.
- Listens to others to fully understand.
- Recognizes the power in the group versus the individual action. Unifies and mobilizes.
- Constantly looking elsewhere for ideas to be learned, copied, and shamelessly borrowed.

Toward the organizational common cause. Never to themselves.

- Grounded and missional with the cause.
- Translates and executes applications toward the cause.
- Enables others to move the cause forward.
- Lets leaders lead.

- Consistently delivers. Not flashy, but reliable.

Here are some cultural leadership perspectives to help shape your organizational culture. Whether you are the most senior person or simply trying to shape culture in your team, these examples of what our leaders did may be useful.

Living out Our United Culture before it was created. Janet, mentioned earlier in Trail Marker #11, served as an executive vice president for UHG over a twenty-five-year career in roles ranging from UnitedHealthcare CEO, strategic relationships, and chief nursing officer. She also volunteered to be in our first group of culture facilitators. Janet's stellar reputation became even more pronounced when we articulated our new values in 2010, about fifteen years after she had already been living them. Janet is one of the most gracious people I know, and she always kept her wits about her, no matter the situation.

Near the end of her career, when we were recognizing her cultural leadership contributions, we asked her fellow 250 culture facilitators for six words to describe Janet. Our CEO chose to participate with, "I can do it in five: 'the soul of the organization!'"[58]

Janet demonstrated what it meant to be a culture practitioner in many respects, including providing balanced feedback to our CEO. In one story, she related how he was clear with her that he didn't agree with her feedback on his handling of a situation. But, after rereading her synopsis of it and thinking it through, he acknowledged its accuracy and asked for her assistance.

Translating Our United Culture to engage specific populations. Dr. Ryan also served in a variety of senior executive roles, with his last one being that of UHG's chief medical officer. Ryan was an original member of our CLT and one of the seventy-seven lead executives who became grounded through the culture workshops and affirmed the core values being rolled out.

Ryan did a great job of taking the newly minted core values and translating them into language specific to clinicians throughout the organization to make them even more effective. Note: he wasn't replacing them with his own language, but he was enhancing and personalizing them through a clinical lens.

He also masterfully articulated how the core values equate to the DNA of the organization at multiple Culture Ambassador Summits. His public addresses always combined his vocational competence, the core values, and the business outcome logic for utilizing Our United Culture.

Ran with Our United Culture to achieve momentum and mass. As I shared in Trail Marker #11, Peter, Andrew, and Mary created the culture ambassador approach. With little to no support from any infrastructure, they voluntarily led our culture ambassadors for the first three years of that community's existence.

They are the epitome of my definition of a cultural leader, in no small part because they literally created what leading a huge group of volunteers actually meant. While holding down their extremely demanding full-time day jobs, they believed enough in Our United Culture to prioritize and innovate what the culture ambassadors could become.

Their roles morphed many times over the three years they led the community, and they met multiple hardships and challenges as the community's volunteer leaders. They never backed away from them, but always optimistically waded into the fray, whether it was organizational turf-related or just breaking down our core values further into usable applications.

Their example paved the way for our other culture ambassador leads who later served in this role. These leaders led with courage and tenacity to fuel the movement; their service was invaluable, and I learned a lot from them.

As with many true leaders, I never had to ask them to lead—they simply led.

One senior leader developed a habit in his presentations of telling the audience what something was—and what something was not. At first, I thought it was repetitive until I realized the different lenses offered different interpretations (of course).

With this cultural leader definition and perspectives of how I saw leaders put it into action, I thought it might also be useful to be clear about what a cultural leader is not. Becoming a cultural leader goes against many of the things most organizations are set up to recognize and reward. Cultural leaders do not:

- Necessarily sit at the highest compensation level
- Always possess the most technical competence
- Avoid displaying vulnerability or transparency
- Decline to ask for help
- Think something "must be created here"
- Exert too much power or control
- Emphasize self over the organization
- Assume the most senior positions represent the best leaders
- Believe they're the smartest people in the room

- Manage with fear and intimidation
- Over-rely on the 6Ps
- Mistreat culture shaping as a strategic priority
- Choke off resources to apply and reinforce culture
- Delegate culture so far down in the organization that it becomes almost invisible
- Lead with pithy statements or flavors of the month
- Stray from being grounded in their core

Positional leadership does not translate to cultural leadership.

In other words, leaders whose position says they should be the best at leading have many times attained a senior position through their technical expertise, developing relationships with a key decision-maker, or through political connivance.

They don't naturally merit any followers.

Leaders who lead the belief system won't necessarily be the same leaders who have gotten the organization's financial results so far. You need to tap into any leader who can believe and be inspired to get the extra out of others to go to the next level within the organization. The enterprise might not fully understand or appreciate the skills these leaders bring to the table, and at the same time, it may start to decipher which historical results are not being accomplished in a way that's healthy for the organization.

On the other hand, positional leadership is everything. Thus the paradox. If people in the organizational construct don't see leaders above them living out the core values, they will not be certain that it is the prescribed behaviors and thinking they are supposed to demonstrate. And of course, they will then lose faith.

We saw this occur repeatedly, in every workshop, with people asking, "Has my leader been through this workshop?" They didn't see evidence of character transformation from their leaders.

As pointed out earlier, some leaders come from where you least expect. Say yes to them and allow them to lead. Don't hinge cultural advancement only on positional leaders.

Probably the best illustration we discovered on leading culture transformation within a large organization showed up within a video, "How to Start a Movement—Leadership Lessons from Dancing Guy" by JV Info Green.[59] This three-minute video was shot spontaneously amidst a throng of people at a waterfront park. The video shows a guy starting to dance, and these leadership lessons are shared:

- A leader needs the guts to stand alone and look ridiculous.
- A leader must be easy to follow and nurture the followers.
- A leader must treat the followers as equals, making everything about the movement.
- The first follower transforms the lone nut into a leader.
- If the leader is flint, then the first follower is the spark that ignites the movement.
- The second follower is the turning point. It is proof that the first follower has done well.
- A movement must be public. Outsiders must see more than just the leader.
- There's no leader or movement without the first followers.

We shared this video at our first Culture Ambassador Summit. We wanted to ensure our people could visually see these leadership principles at work. We didn't want to create "legions of leaders" as much as we wanted enthusiastic "first followers" who would take up the mantle of Our United Culture:

- get grounded in it,
- run with it, and
- see how it could take on a life of its own.

They became cultural leaders.

Questions To Consider

1. How have you seen cultural leadership being exhibited within your organization?
2. How does the definition of cultural leadership resonate with you? Could you see it being applied in your organization with leaders?
3. Which cultural leadership perspective resonated with you the most and why?
4. Could the Dancing Guy video illustration be useful in your organization? If so, how?

Trail Marker #18

Brass Tacks On Culture-Shaping

I'm hopeful you've found the Trail Markers from our culture journey helpful so far. There are so many other examples and topics to cover, but I thought sharing with you some of the frequently asked questions (FAQs) we consistently received over the years of culture shaping at UnitedHealth Group might be useful. I'm highlighting these in case I didn't get to what's on your mind in the previous chapters. Here are the top questions we frequently receive.

1. *Has my leader been to this workshop? What I see in his/her behavior doesn't line up with what I've been hearing over the past two-day workshop.*

Most of the time we encountered this question, the leader referenced had indeed already been to the workshop. We didn't take the time at that moment to research specific people, but instead, we turned the focus back to what the workshop was about—each individual's inside-out transformation. In our workshop discussion on accountability, we kept pointing to our culture principle of "What more can you do to get a different result?"

2. *Why don't we just let go of all the people with bad behavior, so we can more quickly get our culture aligned?*

As you can imagine, this is not as easy as it sounds. (Although I have to admit that question crossed my mind more than once.) And yes, we occasionally do need to terminate people who consistently demonstrate a lack of adherence to Our United Culture. Most of the time, however, it's difficult to decipher whether a pattern of behavior needs remediation or accidental missteps need to be addressed, but with a large dose of grace applied.

I encountered this firsthand through a breakfast meeting I had with one executive (Exec A) who was fired up about the lack of support another executive (Exec B) was demonstrating for Our United Culture. I was taken by surprise, because, in my opinion, Exec B (being berated) was an exemplary example for our people in demonstrating Our United Culture.

Little did Exec A know, I had lunch scheduled with Exec B the same day. As Exec B and I conversed, he brought up complaints against Exec A. Unbeknownst to him, his complaints were almost identical to what Exec A had said about him.

So here are two senior-level executives at UnitedHealth Group, both complaining about each other. Both, from my perspective, were very effective not only in demonstrating Our United Culture but leading it with others as well.

That experience reaffirmed for me how difficult it is for the leader of any organization to ascertain what is truth and what is hearsay.

Of course, I had a solution for that well beyond the performance management scope of our culture office. The answer? Select a large sample size of senior executives in the organization and survey them with two simple questions:

A. Who are the three executives you think consistently *do not* demonstrate Our United Culture?

B. Who are the three executives you think consistently *do* demonstrate Our United Culture?

As with any survey, knowing there could be wide variance in the answers, I wouldn't take any action upon its results. However, it gives the CEO some insight into where to look for fire because he has at least been exposed to the smoke.

3. *What do I do if I consistently notice a colleague or peer not living out our core values?*

This question came up so many times that we developed thirteen steps to take, utilizing the core values and principles of Our United Culture. The first seven steps deal with first looking at yourself. The second six steps have to do with your filters in observing the supposed violator of Our United Culture to ensure you're getting a balanced view of the situation. You can see the tool we developed in appendix 4.

4. *What are we doing to proactively hold leaders accountable for living out Our United Culture?*

Our first response to this question did not prove to be satisfying to our employee base. We suggested, again using our culture principles, have the natural work team encourage the culture principles. First, by approaching the leader one-on-one to make them aware of what the employee group sees. If that approach doesn't take root, consider having two or three employees meet with the leader to explain the observations, thereby calling their behavior into question.

We vastly underestimated the power of the position and retaliation that people feared in this response.

We then proposed a different performance-management assessment tool be used, incorporating the "how" of our values being applied, along with the "what" was being done to recognize the performance of the business objectives being achieved.

5. *How do you address executives treating Our United Culture as a platform, program, or process, rather than seeing it as the character of the organization that should be integrated within everything they do?*

First, we continued to point to Our United Culture as simply "the way we want things done around here." It was a never-ending virtuous cycle where we constantly pointed to the need for "real work" to be done and not treating Our United Culture as an "add-on."

Second, we developed principles workshops (see Trail Marker #15), which included the initial culture principles and core values from the first workshop, along with some additional principles to help the businesses solve ongoing issues with which they had been wrestling.

At first, this approach worked extraordinarily well, with rave reviews coming in from senior executives experiencing breakthrough solutions on some of their most stubborn challenges.

However, the time investment of six hours with a team of people completely went against the grain of the typical problem-solving method most senior leaders used: flip through a PowerPoint, state a bias for action, and then the team dutifully trots off to execute on that bias.

Once again, we had trouble with accountability and the pressures of the urgent taking priority over more insightful, longer-term solutions being developed.

6. *How did you deal with business functions that wanted to take ownership of Our United Culture?*

Thankfully, our CEO made it clear that no one but the businesses should "own" culture. The culture office directly served the office of the CEO. Additionally, because the culture ambassadors were individual volunteers, as were the culture facilitators, those two groups, as informal communities, were not subject to the traditional compliance filtered grids from HR, marketing, communication, and legal that applied to the businesses and functions. Thus, we could operate more freely without going through additional reviews, which enabled us to move more quickly and cut through bureaucratic layers for change.

In the nine years I was in this role, we never had a serious issue develop, although the business functions were at times out of sorts with some changes occurring through empowered culture ambassadors and facilitators.

7. *How can we go faster to get the word out about Our United Culture?*

As with any approach, constraints of time and resources always apply. When we first started the workshops, we were not sure how well they would work. Once we saw how effective they were with participants, we started moving as quickly as possible to scale; however, with our company at the time numbering 140,000 people, there was only so much that could be done.

We asked each workshop participant to share the information as best they could with their teams, and in fact, that was encouraged for their accountability. We also urged the functions to spread the word through whatever channels they could about Our United Culture. Additionally, our CEO championed Our United Culture, regularly reinforcing through all the touchpoints he had with the enterprise.

As volunteers and momentum grew, we could expand the reach of Our United Culture further and faster than ever before. The culture ambassadors were heavily to thank, along with the culture facilitators lending their weight as senior executives to the transformation.

Part of our hesitancy about speed was due to our desire to ensure Our United Culture didn't become a campaign or fall into the trap of just relying on the 6Ps. We wanted people to experience and personally appropriate Our United Culture, not just grab on to slogans, mugs, or T-shirts.

We wanted them to be grounded in their individual, inside-out transformation, so they could help others see the opportunity for personal change and development. We believed that approach was the only true course for organizational transformation.

8. *Did you ever consider changing the core values? How often should they be updated?*

When we first rolled out the five core values for Our United Culture, our CEO was careful to refer to them as Version 1.0. He wanted flexibility for change when we received feedback from our employee base as the core values rolled out. Because the core values had been put together by a small group of senior executives, we wanted to be nimble to shift with the feedback coming in from the general employee population.

Within six months of rollout, it was clear the core values and the more detailed definitions of what we believe, what we value, and how we should behave were here to stay.

To add further reinforcement behind Our United Culture, at the first ambassador summit, our CEO made clear we were in the beginning of a thirty-year journey with Our United Culture. He wanted the core values to truly be our core and to use them to address everything in our organization through a full-blown transformation. That stayed consistent for the nine years I served in the culture office.

During my tenure, there were occasional inquiries to seek shifting one of our values or shifting the language within our core values. The few times that occurred, we demonstrated how the existing values could be used to cover the individual's or group's suggestions.

9. *How much does all of this culture stuff cost? Isn't it expensive to do the things you described in the earlier chapters?*

Yes, it is not an effort for the faint-hearted regarding time and resources. However, in the calculations of what was invested in actual dollars spent, and the value of the hours invested, the total came to less than one-tenth of one percent of UnitedHealth Group's net income. Given the size of UnitedHealth Group, you can see a large number. However, even in a company with one hundred people and revenues of $8 million, all this is possible with thoughtful, intentional leadership when combined with a determination to stay the course.

The challenge, of course, as mentioned in Trail Marker #2, is that it is impossible to hardwire an ROI with this investment of time and resources. The intangibles are too great to pin down other than what is a direct and indirect cost, according to the general ledger.

That said, if you subscribe to Simon Sinek's "Law of Diffusion," you may recall he states that inevitably the conclusion of the law will be reached, but no one can forecast the time span it will take to settle fully.[60]

If you were to view his February 2020 video on this topic, he lists off key ingredients for the law to take place. Every one of those ingredients was utilized by us within the Our United Culture transformation.

10. *Can I, as an employee within my organization, lead culture transformation without the support of the CEO?*

For the overall organization, no. The CEO's support is absolutely vital for wholesale organizational change to occur.

That said, I believe every individual can make a difference within their sphere of influence, no matter how big the organization. Please refer to Trail Marker #17, where leadership can take a variety of forms with many different meaningful results.

11. *How important is recognition to a culture transformation?*

Critically important.

Whether a recognition platform, similar to the one we rolled out to all employees, a "Values Day" celebrated by various businesses, or whether one of the core values takes on a persona to be celebrated across the entire company similar to what our innovation group did with UnitedHealth Group's Innovation Day, every bit of recognition to individuals, teams, and groups makes a difference in the reinforcement of core values.

The beautiful thing about core values recognition is that everyone can win. One group or individual is not put down at the expense of another. Everyone has an equal opportunity to serve others through the organization's core values.

12. *How should executive incentives be aligned with the core values transformation?*

Every employee should be crystal clear about how their incentive will be determined. Otherwise, what's the point of the incentive? You'll never truly get the results you're looking for unless you are clear about what is expected.

I look at the core values as the "how" an organization operates. As mentioned in FAQ #4, the "how" should be clear along with the "what" on business objectives. Both should be evaluated separately and clearly.

Several other organizations have been successful in clarifying portions of their incentives around their values. In the book *Built on Values,* Anne Rhoades lays out a terrific approach to fully align core values with employee compensation. I believe incentives should first be driven at the company level, determined by whether overall organizational goals/targets have been attained. Next, at a group level, say at the business division or segment level, with their organizational goals/targets. Lastly, the individual employee level.

The pay transparency laws we're now beginning to see are a wonderful start toward supporting the capitalistic system we've benefitted from for years here in America, while making strides to advance opportunities for the broader employee base.

13. *How do you leverage the core values transformation into other meaningful platforms, programs, and processes within the organization?*

Using a Values Lens as the filter for your reassessment is the easiest answer to this question. The 6Ps are critically necessary to advance business solutions; however, if set apart from the core values due to pride of authorship/ownership, control, or even a lack of understanding, the 6Ps will inevitably become a flavor of the month and drift away.

The core values cultural transformation should enable the 6Ps to be even more effective than they would be as a standalone, given you are utilizing the organization's DNA to advance them forward. They become an outgrowth of the core versus a "dangling participle" with no serious juice in them.

14. *What is the difference between employee engagement and corporate culture?*

I like the way Deloitte defines the difference: "Culture is a system of values, beliefs, and behaviors that shapes how actual work gets done—the way things work around here. In contrast, engagement is about employees' level of commitment to the organization and their work—how people feel about the way things work around here."[61]

Employee engagement is one component of measuring corporate culture, but not the total end-game metric. At UnitedHealth Group, our CEO looked at the trinity of employee engagement, net promoter score, and earnings per share as a rough metric of how well Our United Culture was grounded within our organization. And no, we didn't create a confluence of the three measures; we kept them separate.

Questions To Consider

1. Which FAQ struck you the most?

2. What other questions come to mind so far?

Epilogue

What I've Realized In Writing This Book

Ted Lasso is an AppleTV drama about an American football coach hired to lead a British futbol (soccer) team. He is an amazingly unique individual who strives to put his players first, believing positive results will follow.

In one episode, his team, AFC Richmond, had just initiated a strategy Ted called "total futbol," where the players don't have any assigned positions or roles. Instead, they work together as a fluid, seamless unit to score the ball into the opponent's goal.

Despite losing the game, the team played wonderfully together in the second half as they grasped more fully what Ted was asking them to do. After the game, a journalist named Trent Crimm, who had been traveling with the team all year, rushed up to Ted, overly giddy with excitement. Ted doesn't have a clue what Trent is excited about:

Trent: Ted, it's going to work!

Ted: Great. (puzzled) What is?

Trent: Total futbol!

Ted: OK.

Trent: And I'll tell you why.

Ted: Why?

Trent: The Lasso Way. You haven't switched tactics in a week.

Ted: I haven't?

Trent: No. You've done this over three seasons!

Ted: I have?

Trent: Yes, where slowly but surely building a club-wide culture of trust and support through thousands of imperceptible moments all leading to their inevitable conclusion: total futbol!!

Ted: Well, how about that?! (still puzzled)

Trent: Eeeaah!! It's gonna work!!![62]

"Thousands of imperceptible moments" build cultures. Family, corporate, and societal. Sure, some situations are easier than others to highlight and punctuate, but a living, breathing organism filled with human "beings" is impossible to specifically pinpoint exactly what input created which output. Like parenting and cultivating, so many distinct actions are necessary, but what specifically yields the desired outcome is a mystery.

Many times, hindsight is the necessary insight gained to more clearly see the way forward.

My culture journey as a practitioner is no different. After my employment at UHG, I've come to realize even more ingredients and blends to give better results. In addition to the eighteen trail markers I just shared, I noticed a pattern emerging that leveraged DURAM (see

Trail Marker #4) and gave rise to SPARK—a shorthand acronym I use as a framework to ignite and fuel lasting business results.

S—Specifically define. Even with what we thought we had defined well in our core values with beliefs, values, and behaviors, we still found people tossing phrases around with a desire for different types of cultures. Well-meaning, but dilution occurred at times, causing fractures and inefficiency with our objectives.

P—Personally appropriate. A transformed character transforms culture. Until individual change occurs, which originates from beliefs, which influences thinking, which creates new behaviors, the results won't change. Each individual within the organization needs to intentionally decide what to take and apply from the organizational culture to their personal life. Linkage and collective alignment are key.

A—Accountably apply. Our walk must talk louder than our talk talks. No matter how we've defined it and what we say we will appropriate for ourselves, unless we apply it, it's all glow and no show. *Intentional, deliberate, disciplined,* and *purposeful* are all words that describe "how" application should occur.

R—Rigorously reinforce. Consistently and clearly doubling down on the emphasis you have with your core values takes a lot of thoughtful work. But it's more than just a rinse-and-repeat process; it's synergistic and interdependent with accountability applied, again and again and again.

K—Keep it fresh. While the core values must remain just that, if they *only* remain that, you'll lose the SPARK. Staying real, real-time, and relevant with fresh, vibrant perspectives and applications keeps people interested, engaged, and striving to drive the core further and deeper into the organization.

Applying SPARK and the leadership necessary to implement it will always be an evolving, difficult, nebulous, ambiguous, and rewarding challenge. As with any challenge you face, are you grounded upon, integrated, and congruent with your core values? If so, no matter what issues confront you, by using your values lens you'll be able to ground yourself and quickly align your organization with clear instructions to deal with it. Your character will shine through.

I'm grateful I heeded the advice of multiple counselors who told me not to rush production of this book. I know the content is different from what it would have been had I tried to complete it sooner.

Since I've stepped away from being employed within a corporate culture, here are a few quicker "ahas" to further reinforce the results I've outlined:

- I met a gentleman named Gerry a while back at a friend's home. We hit it off, and near the end of our conversation, I found out he had started his career with Andersen Consulting. We had the same core values and grounding as we both started at Arthur Andersen immediately out of college. Shared experiences and like-mindedness help speed relationships.
- I also had the opportunity to have lunch with one of my former bosses at Arthur Andersen, Dick. Dick was the Los Angeles office managing partner when the firm imploded, and I hadn't spoken with him in the twenty years since. When I saw Dick, it was as if twenty years hadn't happened, and two and a half hours later, true to the firm's values and Dick's character, he had given generously of his time and offered to assist me in whatever way he could. The relationship we had formed lasted.
- I continue to realize my own character continues to be shaped through life's experiences and my personal core values. How I look

at and approach different challenges results from who I am, not from what others expect. I can affirm my friend Kurt's statement, "There's a different way of being that's more fulfilling, and it just works better."

- Societal culture is charged with polarization. Everyone has an opinion, and we seem to have lost the ability to be truly curious and listen to one another. Being grounded with my personal core values helps me major on the majors and minor on the minors. Applying SPARK, in my personal and family life (without announcement, of course), has proven to be worthwhile.

Lasting results can never be measured, but they can be forever known.

A transformed character transforms culture. It's simple, but not easy.

One person, one day, one step at a time.

The ending of this trail is just your beginning and should never end.

Ignore this at your own peril.

Let's go get 'em!

Gratitudes

Similar to workplace culture, personal character is shaped by many people and a myriad of life experiences. I'm grateful for many people who have touched my life, but specifically for this manuscript, I owe particular gratitude to:

My Savior and Lord, Jesus Christ, who has given me much. I'm still grasping this truth from John 3:27, "A man can receive nothing unless it has been given to him from heaven." And for the Holy Scriptures, the foundational divining rod for all human character.

My wife, Carrie, and our children, who have offered unending encouragement and support, along with continually sharpening my character, amidst all my idiosyncrasies, as we shape our growing family culture. The mirror you provide for my personal character development is invaluable.

My friend, John Blumberg, who kept telling me, "The book will come out when the book is supposed to come out." How true and encouraging, along with insightful wisdom from his ongoing practice of integrity.

My co-laborer at Crossroads Career, Brian Ray, for decades of sharpening content and character development through our weekly chats.

My friend and former colleague, Matt Peterson. Without your savvy guidance and support, I would not have lasted at UnitedHealth Group long enough to have both gained the opportunity and lasted through the experience.

My fellow UnitedHealth Group culture facilitators and ambassadors, who selflessly served our organization and blessed me in many different ways. The lessons shared so far, with more to come, stem from your efforts and contributions.

My friends in the UnitedHealth Group Culture Office, particularly Leisa Carston and Brad Wiggins, who helped me navigate through the bulk of the nine-year journey. Thank you for steadily serving so many characters in your roles, particularly me.

My friends at Indie Books International. Without your guidance, patience, creativity, attention to detail, and endurance in this journey with me, this book never would have unfolded to be what it is today.

About The Author

Dave Sparkman is the founder and managing director of SPARK Your Culture, a workplace culture advisory services firm, focused on helping organizations transform and flourish through healthy, high-performance cultures.

In his corporate career, Dave served as the SVP, Culture at UnitedHealth Group, a Fortune 5 public company based in Minnetonka, Minnesota. Over nine years in that role, he led efforts to infuse an over three-hundred-thousand-person organization with a corporate mission and values that would improve results, including the customer and employee experience.

Prior to UnitedHealth Group, Dave lived in Los Angeles and served as the West Region Partner, People, at Arthur Andersen, a worldwide audit, tax, and consulting firm.

He also currently serves as the volunteer executive director and board chair for Crossroads Career, a faith-based, job-transition ministry dedicated to helping people who are unemployed or unfulfilled.

Dave and his wife, Carrie, reside in Minnesota. They enjoy spending time with their four adult children, their three spouses, and a growing brood of seven grandchildren.

You can contact Dave through email at
Dave@SPARKYourculture.com.

Appendix 1

UnitedHealth Group Values Brochure—Our United Culture

In addition to the introductory memo from Robert mentioned on page 11, here are UnitedHealth Group's five core values, along with our initial view of measuring success, introduced on June 8, 2010.

Integrity

Honor commitments. Never compromise ethics.

We believe: We must be an enterprise that represents the highest level of personal and institutional integrity. With integrity, people and institutions will want to work with us, and our core purpose will not be compromised.

We value integrity: We will honor commitments. We will never compromise ethics. We will be known for living to the highest forms and standards of ethical behavior. We will make honest commitments and consistently honor those commitments.

We behave: We will speak the truth. We will deliver on our promises. We will have the courage to acknowledge mistakes and do whatever is needed to address them.

Compassion

Walk in the shoes of people we serve and those with whom we work.

We believe: In order to achieve the full potential of our enterprise and its purpose, to *Help People Live Healthier Lives*, we must fully understand and align with their needs and realities.

We value compassion: We will walk in the shoes of people we serve and those with whom we work. We celebrate our role in serving people and society in an area so vitally human as their health. We must be truly compassionate and genuinely understand, feel, and identify with their needs.

We behave: We will actively listen to fully understand and genuinely empathize with people's realities. We will then respond in service and advocacy for each individual, each group or community, and for society as a whole.

Relationships

Build trust through collaboration.

We believe: In order to achieve the full potential of our enterprise in our efforts to help people by *Making Healthcare Work for Everyone*, we understand and believe that we can never achieve that goal alone. We must positively engage the efforts and interests of everyone who has been touched by and can contribute to that effort.

We value relationships: We will build trust through collaboration in order to take action and find solutions. We understand that relationships are critical to help people work together, even when their interests are not fully aligned or fulfilled. We realize relationships bind people in organizations through trust. Trust is earned and preserved through truthfulness, integrity, and active engagement in collaboration with our colleagues and clients.

We behave: We will approach all people with respect, humility, confidence, and energy. We will confront issues, not people. When we have differences, we will confront them in a direct way, not passively, to resolve the issues that drive those differences. We will actively engage with people and institutions to share information, ideas, and resources in order to help others achieve their goals. We will encourage the variety of thoughts and perspectives that reflect the diversity of our markets, customers, and workforce.

Innovation

Invent the future and learn from the past.

We believe: Our fundamental role is to *Make Healthcare Work for Everyone*. The healthcare environment must be engaged in constant change, yet embody a positive dynamic—it must change progressively. In turn, we must be thoughtful and advocates of such change. We must value and be proficient at adapting to change as we pursue a course of continuous, positive, and practical innovation as a core competency within our enterprise.

We value innovation: We will learn from experiences of the past and use those insights to invent a better future to make the healthcare environment work and serve everyone more fairly, productively, and consistently.

We behave: We will continue to respectfully challenge the status quo. We will encourage and invest in new ideas. We will be curious and not afraid to fail in honest efforts to focus on practical and purposeful innovation that builds value and benefits the entire healthcare system—so it truly works for everyone.

Performance

Demonstrate excellence in everything we do.

We believe: The challenges of healthcare are great. Yet they are matched only by the opportunities. Our purpose to *Help People live Healthier Lives* and our role to *Make Healthcare Work for Everyone* can only be met by demonstrated commitment to and achievement of performance excellence in everything we do.

We value performance: We are committed to deliver and demonstrate excellence in everything we do.

We behave: We will be accountable and responsible for consistently delivering high-quality and superior results that make a difference. We will challenge ourselves to strive for even better outcomes in all key performance areas.

Measuring success

We will know we're "in culture" through:

A Culture Leadership Team, comprised of selected leaders from each of the businesses and key functional areas on rotational terms, will be accountable to annually oversee the production and assessment of:

- A Values Index drawn from external surveys (member, employer, broker, provider, and possibly government)
- An Employee Cultural Index drawn from employee surveys

- An Executive Values Leadership Index drawn from our annual 360 review process

The Culture Leadership Team will be responsible to ensure alignment of our systems and processes to reflect this new culture. They will also be responsible for an annual report on cultural strength and alignment with related current year results and comparative year-over-year analysis.

Our Mission Is To Help People Live Healthier Lives.
Our Role Is To Make Healthcare Work For Everyone.
Our Collective Leadership Will Guide The Way Forward.

The seventy-seven names of the senior leaders present are on the back of this brochure to memorialize their commitment to Our United Culture.

Appendix 2

UnitedHealth Group Culture Principles—Our United Culture

- How can I enable more innovation?
  Wheelbarrow Hint: Stay Curious
- Where am I on the energy dial?
  Energy Hint: Manage my energy
- How can I better manage my busy mind?
  Be Here Now Hint: At work and at home
- How big of a team am I playing on?
  Broken Squares Hint: How I play the game matters
- At what level am I truly listening?
  Five Levels Of Listening Hint: Listen to understand
- What shadow am I casting?
  Leadership Shadow Hint: What I do and permit is what I promote

- Where am I on the mood elevator?
  Mood Elevator Hint: Get to curious
- Am I taking time to understand?
  People With Empty Thoughts Hint: Assume positive intent
- What thinking is driving my behavior?
  Results Cone Hint: Insights can shift my thinking
- How can I shape culture?
  DURAM Circle Hint: Use DURAM
- How would this look through a different lens?
  Our Values Lens Hint: Bring new possibilities to bear
- Am I keeping different behavioral styles in mind?
  Four Styles Hint: All styles get results
- What more can I do to get different results?
  Accountability Ladder Hint: Climb the accountability ladder
- How certain am I of the answer?
  F Hint: Remember to count the Fs
- Is this the best use of my time and energy?
  Blue Chips Hint: Focus on my blue chips
- How can I coach to enable insights and get results?
  Keyhole With Words In It Hint: Use insight-based coaching
- When am I at my best?
  Up Button On Elevator Hint: When I'm up the Mood Elevator
- How can I help my team get fulfilling results?
  Dart Hitting Bull's Eye Hint: Share appreciation and feedback

- How can I be even more effective in my thinking?
  Left Brain Right Brain Hint: Use both sides of the brain

- Am I spending time on gravity issues?
  Control/Influence/Beyond Influence Hint: Focus on what I can control or influence

- Do I truly understand the best way to support you?
  How Can I Support You? Hint: Ask often to truly understand

- How can our values shape my approach?
  Compass For What/How Hint: Use our values to lead the what and the how

- How are my filters affecting my viewpoint?
  How I Perceive People, Situations, Events Hint: Things are not always as they appear to me

- What's a simple way to manage my time?
  5 Hint: Finish with Five

Appendix 3

Culture Dissonance Recommendations

Theme #1–Set Expectations:

Publish enterprise goals and leadership expectations for clarity of direction and accountability

- Enterprise Goals—Declare and cascade our enterprise goals through the businesses to enable our leaders to get their organization's goals aligned
- Leadership Profile 2.0—Set the bar for all leaders that comes with the privilege we have and the responsibility we must own to fulfill our mission

Theme #2–Measure Behaviors:

Evaluate the "how" as importantly as the "what" to make expectations stick

- The "What" and "How"—Require the performance review process to evaluate employees on values-based behaviors and our leaders on the traits Leadership Profile 2.0 stipulates

- Leadership Shadow Index—Evaluate leaders specifically on how their direct reports view their behaviors by looking at a confluence of employee engagement indices

Theme #3—Listen to Feedback:

Gather feedback to help employees feel heard and to give leaders behavior development input

- Two-Way Feedback Channels—Require that leaders facilitate more two-way feedback channels, listening forums, and follow-up action plans between leaders and their employees
- Peer Feedback Survey—Create a short, non-punitive survey tool required by all leaders that gives them input from peers and directs for personal leadership development

Theme #4—Reward Behaviors:

Align enterprise incentives and be explicit about performance and reward linkages

- Single Enterprise bonus plan—Align the enterprise by motivating "better together" behaviors via a single bonus plan funding rate with CEO discretion on participation rates and holdbacks
- Individual Rewards Statement—Publish an individual crosswalk of performance review results to rewards for all employees that explicitly outlines the math and judgments used in the calculations

Theme #5—Celebrate Our Results:

Nurture the drive our employees have to fulfill our mission and find ways for more to share in our success

- Mission Event—Promote our mission success by hosting an event that highlights the specific ways in which we help people live healthier lives or make the system simpler
- Success Sharing—Promote Employee Stock Purchase Plan and/or explore other options that have a lower cost buy-in so all employees can share in the financial wins of the Enterprise

Appendix 4

What To Do If Someone Isn't Living Out The Values (In Your Opinion)

Not Living the Values? Context, context, context.

Self-Awareness

___ Is your observation a pattern of behavior or an isolated incident?

___ Am I above Curious?

___ What Fs might I be missing?

___ Is my Values Lens fully at work?

___ What do I think they were thinking?

___ What more could I have done to get a different result?

___ What is my motivation for taking action?

Action: Platinum Rule—Do unto others as they want to be done unto

___ Relationship with them? Credibility translation to trust?

___ Timing approach and tone: I feel you could be even more effective

___ How do you want them to remember the conversation? Grateful?

___ Confront the situation—Time is the enemy of conflict

___ Escalate if needed

___ Deal with any damage without throwing people under the bus

"Be the change you want to see in the world."
Gandhi

"Bad decisions can't be undone, but they can be redeemed."
Dr. Erwin Lutzer

Endnotes

1 Shawn Tully, "Can UnitedHealth Really Fix The System?" *Fortune*, May 6, 2013, https://fortune.com/2013/05/06/can-unitedhealth-really-fix-the-system/.

2 John P. Kotter & James L. Heskett, *Corporate Culture and Performance* (Free Press, 1992).

3 Catherine Schenkel, "Take Your Culture Off Cruise Control", CPHR Manitoba, September 25, 2017, https://www.cphrmb.ca/news/367293/Take-your-Culture-Off-Cruise-Control.htmTrail.

4 Simon Sinek, "What Should Your Company Culture Be? Start With Verbs." *Big Think+*, September 13, 2019. https://bigthink.com/plus/simon-sinek-define-your-company-culture-using-verbs-not-nouns/.

5 Edgar H. Schein, *Organizational Culture and Leadership: A dynamic view* (San Francisco: Jossey-Bass, 1985, 1992), 6–7.

6 David Shanklin, Culture IQ, as quoted by Melissa Ramos; https://howtoworkwell.com/blogs/features/cultureiq.

7 Carolyn Taylor, "A culture of simplicity: Keeping it simple, the smart way," March 30, 2016. https://www.humansynergistics.com/blog/culture-university/2016/03/30/a-culture-of-simplicity-keeping-it-simple-the-smart-way/.

8 Benjamin Laker, "Culture Is A Company's Single Most Powerful Advantage. Here's Why," *Forbes*, April 23, 2021, https://www.forbes.com/sites/benjaminlaker/2021/04/23/culture-is-a-companys-single-most-powerful-advantage-heres-why/.

9 John Shufelt, "Why Engaged Employees Are Necessary," *Forbes Books*, December 22, 2022, https://books.forbes.com/author-articles/why-engaged-employees-are-necessary/.

10 Simon Reynolds, "Lessons You Can Learn From Apple's CEO," *Forbes*, March 25, 2015, https://www.forbes.com/sites/siimonreynolds/2015/03/25/lessons-you-can-learn-from-apples-ceo/.

11 Dina Dwyer Owens, "Values: Look At What Your Actions Tell People," GrowthInstitute.com, accessed August 15, 2025, https://www.dinadwyerowens.com/blog/2016/october/values-look-at-what-your-actions-tell-people/.

12 "10 Proven Methods For Measuring The ROI Of Company Culture," *Forbes*, December 16, 2019, https://www.forbes.com/councils/forbeshumanresourcescouncil/2019/12/16/10-proven-methods-for-measuring-the-roi-of-company-culture/.

13 Robert [Anonymized], UnitedHealth Group, 2013, as recorded by Dave Sparkman from internal documents/notes.

14 Attributed to Yogi Berra, https://www.socratic-method.com/quote-meanings/yogi-berra-if-you-dont-know-where-you-are-going-you-might-wind-up-someplace-else.

15 Larry Senn & Jim Hart, *Winning Teams Winning Cultures* (Senn Delaney, 2006).

16 Carl Rogers, *On Becoming a Person: A Therapist's View of Psychotherapy* (HarperOne,1995), Kindle locations 4283–4290.

17 Maya Angelou. https://www.socratic-method.com/quote-meanings-and-interpretations/maya-angelou-ive-learned-that-people-will-forget-what-you-said-people-will-forget-what-you-did-but-people-will-never-forget-how-you-made-them-feel.

18 Soren Kierkegaard, *Fear and Trembling* (Copenhagen,1843).

19 Pastor Larry Osborne, North Coast Church (Vista, Calif).

20 The Bible, New Living Translation.

21 John Blumberg interview with the author.

22 Jim Collins, *Good to Great: Why Some Companies Make The Leap…and Others Don't* (Harper Business, 2001).

23 "The Power of Words" (video), https://www.youtube.com/watch?v=Hzgzim5m7oU.

24 *Darkest Hour* (film), Joe Wright, director, (Universal Pictures, 2017).

25 Carmine Gallo, 'Darkest Hour' Screenwriter Anthony McCarten On How A Leader's Words Can Change The World." *Forbes*. January 3, 2018, https://www.forbes.com/sites/carminegallo/2018/01/03/darkest-hour-screenwriter-anthony-mccarten-on-how-a-leaders-words-can-change-the-world/.

26 Margaret Thatcher Foundation, "Remarks on The American Model (The Heritage Foundation)," *Margaret Thatcher Foundation*. Note: This quote comes from a speech she delivered at The Heritage Foundation in Washington, D.C., on September 26, 1991, titled "America, An Idea." The Margaret Thatcher Foundation provides the full transcript of her remarks.

27 G.K. Chesterton, *What I Saw in America* (New York: Dodd, Mead and Company, 1922).

28 "Detroit Defied Reality to Help Win World War II," *USO*, December 20, 2015.

29 "From 'Will It Run?' to National Museum," *USO*, September 26, 2015.

30 *Merriam-Webster.com Dictionary*, "faith," accessed August 26, 2025, https://www.merriam-webster.com/dictionary/faith, and "belief," accessed August 26, 2025, https://www.merriam-webster.com/dictionary/belief.

31 Robert [Anonymized], UnitedHealth Group, 2013, as recorded by Dave Sparkman. Internal documents/notes.

32 C.S. Lewis, *Mere Christianity* (New York: Touchstone, a division of Simon & Schuster, 1996), 125.

33 Matthew McConaughey, "Matthew McConaughey Motivational Speech Transcript," https://speakola.com/grad/matthew-mcconaughey-13-truths-2015, May 15, 2015.

34 *The Imitation Game* (film), directed by Morten Tyldum (Los Angeles: The Weinstein Company, 2014).

35 Adam Grant, quoted in "Team," *Marvel Medical Staffing*, accessed July 14, 2025, https://marvelmedstaff.com/team/.

36 Dawn Arnevik, UnitedHealth Group, 2015, as recorded by Dave Sparkman from internal documents/notes.

37 Robert [Anonymized], UnitedHealth Group, 2011, handwritten note on a letter to the author.

38 Avildsen, J. G. (1984). *The Karate Kid.* Columbia Pictures.

39 Sheryl Skolnick (likely with team), *UnitedHealth Group Incorporated*, Mizuho Securities USA LLC, July 19, 2017, https://www.mizuhogroup.com/binaries/content/assets/pdf/americas/insights/2017/07/unitedhealth_group_incorporated_2017-07-19.pdf.

40 Richard Sheridan, *Joy, Inc.: How We Built a Workplace People Love* (New York: Portfolio/Penguin, 2013).

41 Robert [Anonymized], UnitedHealth Group, 2013, as recorded by the author based on internal notes.

42 Keith Ruth, UnitedHealth Group, 2016, as recorded by the author based on internal notes.

43 B.F. Skinner, *Science and Human Behavior* (New York: The Free Press, 1953), 65.

44 "The Most Popular Sports In The World," *World Atlas*, accessed July 14, 2025, https://www.worldatlas.com/articles/what-are-the-most-popular-sports-in-the-world.html.

45 *Ted Lasso*, season 1, episode 6, "Two Aces," directed by Declan Lowney, written by Jane Becker, teleplay by Jason Sudeikis and Brendan Hunt, aired September 4, 2020, on Apple TV+.

46 Jacob Morgan, "14 Top CEOs Share Their Definition Of 'Leadership,' What's Yours?" *The Future Organization*, August 13, 2020, https://thefutureorganization.com/14-top-ceos-share-their-definition-of-leadership%e2%80%8b-whats-yours/.

47 Laura Bouttell, "Inspiring Leadership Quotes That Transform Management Excellence," *Quarterdeck*, June 9, 2025, https://quarterdeck.co.uk/articles/quotes-leadership-and-management#.

48 John C. Maxwell, quoted in "YOUR WALK TALKS—Another IPS," *Life-Built Poems*, accessed July 14, 2025, https://lifebuiltpoems.com/your-walk-talks-another-ips/.

49 Admiral Grace Murray Hopper, quoted in John Hamerlinck, "Leaders Versus Managers," *Leading Differently*, January 22, 2015, https://leadingdifferently.com/2015/01/22/leaders-versus-managers/.

50 Lao Tse, Tao Te Ching, quoted in "Leadership—Development of Management Thoughts, Principles and Types," *Inflibnet.ac.in*, accessed July 14, 2025, https://ebooks.inflibnet.ac.in/hrmp02/chapter/291/.

51 Warren Bennis, quoted in "Casting a Shadow that Creates a Winning District," *Ed Elements*, May 28, 2019. https://www.edelements.com/blog/casting-a-shadow-that-creates-a-winning-district.

52 Peter Drucker, quoted in "Business leadership | You may be doing things right, but are you doing the right things?," *HR Grapevine*, November 9, 2022. https://www.hrgrapevine.com/content/article/you-may-be-doing-things-right-but-are-you-doing-the-right-things-servicenow.

53 Rosemarie Perla, "Are You Leading or Taking a Walk Alone?" *Perla Coaching*, accessed July 14, 2025, https://www.perlacoaching.com/blog/are-you-leading-or-taking-a-walk-alone/.

54 Larry Senn and Jim Hart, "What leadership shadow do you cast?" *SmartBrief*, February 24, 2016, https://www.smartbrief.com/original/what-leadership-shadow-do-you-cast#.

55 Senn Delaney, Leadership Shadow Principle tagline.

56 Jon Michael, "Congruent Leadership Is Authentic Leadership," *Forbes*, April 29, 2022, https://www.forbes.com/councils/forbescoachescouncil/2022/04/29/congruent-leadership-is-authentic-leadership/.

57 Matthew Jones, "Congruence Is What Separates the Most Influential Leaders From Everyone Else. Here's Why," *Inc.com*, June 20, 2018, https://www.inc.com/matthew-jones/congruence-is-what-separates-most-influential-leaders-from-everyone-else-heres-why.html.

58 Robert [Anonymized], UnitedHealth Group, 2015. As recalled by the author. Internal documents/notes.

59 JV Info Green, "How to start a Movement—Leadership Lessons from Dancing Guy," YouTube video, 2:56, October 27, 2017.

60 Simon Sinek, *Start With Why: How Great Leaders Inspire Everyone to Take Action* (New York: Portfolio/Penguin, 2011), 78–83.

61 "Leading the social enterprise: Reinvent with a human focus," Deloitte Insights, Deloitte Touche Tohmatsu Limited, 2019 Global Human Capital Trends, February 20, 2020, https://www.deloitte.com/an/en/services/consulting/perspectives/reinvent-with-a-human-focus.html.

62 *Ted Lasso* (TV show), developed by Jason Sudeikis, Apple TV+, United States.

www.ingramcontent.com/pod-product-compliance
Ingram Content Group UK Ltd.
Pitfield, Milton Keynes, MK11 3LW, UK
UKHW021432280726
14060UKWH00001BA/36

9 781966 168782